"Few things are more painful than watching a child walk away from the Lord. In *God's Heart for the Prodigal,* Steve and Jenia Williams write from both scripture and personal experience as the parents of Christian artist Zach Williams. They understand the heartbreak and hope that come with loving a prodigal and the faithfulness of God through it all. Let this family's compelling story be a reminder for you that no one is beyond the reach of God."

—Greg Laurie, senior pastor of
Harvest Christian Fellowship

GOD'S HEART FOR THE PRODIGAL

GOD'S HEART FOR THE PRODIGAL

A DEVOTIONAL JOURNEY OF MERCY, REDEMPTION, AND UNFAILING LOVE

Written by the parents of

ZACH WILLIAMS

STEVE & JENIA WILLIAMS

with ROBERT NOLAND

God's Heart for the Prodigal: A Devotional Journey of Mercy, Redemption, and Unfailing Love

Published by K-LOVE Books, a partner of Forefront Books, Nashville, Tennessee.

Distributed by Simon & Schuster.

Library of Congress Control Number: 2026902981

Print ISBN: 978-1-63763-534-6

E-book ISBN: 978-1-63763-535-3

Cover Design by Greg Jackson, Thinkpen Design
Interior Design by PerfecType, Nashville, TN

Printed in the United States of America

26 27 28 29 30 31 RR4 10 9 8 7 6 5 4 3 2 1

CONTENTS

A WORD FROM ZACH

Following the release of my memoir, *Rescue Story*, and sharing about what the Lord has done in my life, I've had the privilege of hearing from so many readers. One of the primary elements brought to light in the book was the unwavering commitment of my parents, Steve and Jenia Williams (Jenia is pronounced *Jee-nee*). Mom and Dad's deep walk with the Lord, relentless prayers, and ever-present unconditional love and grace for me was a major catalyst that God's Spirit worked through to bring this prodigal back home to Him. That same love and grace also played a part in my wife, Crystal, turning her life over to the Lord around the same time I did. That's also true for my sister, Amy, and her husband, Toby. Today, as a family, we're fully committed to Jesus. While, of course, all glory goes to God, I want to give credit and offer gratitude to my parents for their perseverance on my behalf.

Their journey of faith over the course of more than ten years led me to the concept for this devotional. I wanted to offer Mom and Dad the opportunity to speak to those who are walking through their own prodigal season with a son, daughter, grandchild, spouse, other family member, or friend. Or maybe, just like me for so many years, someone who is struggling and desperately searching for answers, grasping for hope and help. While you'll hear from me and Crystal, the primary voices will be my mom and dad as they share their wisdom, experience, and godly counsel. Because they know what a parent's broken heart feels like. They understand what it means to ask God some tough questions like "What did we do wrong?" And they have the callouses on their knees from years of submitting to the Lord, asking Him to rescue their kids.

Now on the other side, after more than a decade of experiencing God's favor and blessing following His answers to their prayers, they most definitely have something to say and have won the right to be heard. In this devotional, they'll talk honestly about this difficult place in which many find themselves with a loved one. They can speak firsthand with empathy to offer encouragement and inspiration, and they will challenge you to become stronger in your own faith through this difficult season, lifting up your prodigal as you keep watch down the road for him or her to come back home—just like I did.

BEFORE YOU BEGIN

Zach

First, there are three ways to use this devotional:

1. By yourself, just as you would read and engage with any devotional book.
2. With a small group, whether that be at church, in a Bible study, or with Christian friends.
3. In a support group, getting together with others who are walking through life with a prodigal loved one.

Regardless of how you use the book, before you dive in to the first day, here are a few thoughts we hope will help you start strong and finish well in these pages:

Commit to setting aside intentional and undistracted time as you go through each day. If you miss a day or two, don't give in to the temptation to feel any guilt; just jump back in. Commit, never quit.

Choose the best time and place in your day to read and engage. Stay away from distractions like your phone, device, or TV. Find a place where you can be on your own and focus on connecting with God. Your relationship with Jesus and the prayers for your prodigal are worth every moment you invest.

Read and take in *all* the content. We worked hard to make every word count, and God certainly did with His Word. So don't scan like you would a text or email; engage each day like reading a personal letter from us, because that's actually what this is. If you prefer to use a different Bible version to read the scriptures, that's great. The point is to connect with God's Word. All Bible verses are italicized to easily distinguish them from the other text.

Application/Discussion Questions are at the end of each day. The purpose of these is to guide you to connect and apply the day's content to your life. The more open and honest you are in your answers, the more opportunity to grow in spiritual maturity. If you go through this devotional with a small group or support group, you can use these questions for discussion.

Here's the format for each day, divided into three sections:

Music—My parents handpicked one of my songs to match up with each day's message. Listening to a song as you start the day can help get your mind and heart into the right space to hear from the Lord, while the lyrics can connect to the topic of the day's content as another way to encourage and inspire you.

Message—This main segment includes a testimony, teaching, and text from Scripture. Here, we share from our hearts some of the truths the Lord has taught us through our own journey.

Reflection—In this segment, there are two questions:

1. The *personal* question is for you to receive from Him. Prayerfully think through and apply the truth of God's Word to your own life.
2. The *prodigal* question is meant to help you process your loved one's story. Apply the truth of God's Word in anticipation of your prodigal's journey back home.

Whether by yourself or with others, we encourage you to write down your answers. Studies have shown that writing can create a stronger, more impactful experience. The questions may also be used for discussion in a small group or support group.

At the end of each day, there is journal space for you to write down anything you believe the Lord is showing you. Or you can use this if you need more space for your answers to the application questions. Jotting down your thoughts, impressions, and God's directives is a great way to process both your feelings and your faith. Journaling is a proven method to help anyone walk through a difficult or even traumatic season.

Pray. Allow time each day to talk with God and tell Him everything. Open up to Him. Listen for His voice in your spirit. Share your heart and speak your mind. Be honest. Be specific. No *thee*s and *thou*s or fancy spiritual language is necessary. Two great scriptures to remember are Psalm 46:10, *"Be still, and know that I am God,"* and the prayer of Samuel in 1 Samuel 3:9, *"Speak, LORD, for your servant is listening."*

Finally, if there are a number of people in your church or Christian community around you who are dealing with a prodigal in their lives, consider starting a support group. Going through the devotional together in a weekly meeting would give you content and direction for thirty meetings. Whether you go through each day in advance or read it aloud in your time together, you can use the questions to discuss and process with one another. The synergy of your prayers for each prodigal could be the most powerful aspect of the group.

As you get started, our prayer is that, by the end of the next thirty days, you will be closer to Jesus and your prodigal will be closer to home.

Jesus looked at them and said,
"With man this is impossible,
but not with God;
all things are possible with God."
(Mark 10:27)

Day 1

The Unconditional Love of the Father

Music

Listen to today's song:

"Far Too Good to a Man like Me"

Steve and Jenia

For the next thirty days, inside these pages, we want to invite you to walk with us for encouragement, inspiration, and growth in your faith and relationship with Jesus. Our prayer is to offer hope and help if you

- Have a son or daughter who has strayed from faith in Christ

- Have a grandson or granddaughter who has strayed from faith in Christ
- Have a spouse who has strayed from faith in Christ
- Have a brother or sister who has strayed from faith in Christ
- Have a close family member who has strayed from faith in Christ
- Have a loved one who seems to have no interest in God
- Are struggling in your own faith and searching for answers

To introduce our title and theme, we'll begin with Jesus's parable in Luke 15 about a prodigal son.

Let's look for His point behind His teaching. Starting with verse 11, He told the story of a father with two sons. One day, the younger son came to his dad and asked for his share of the estate. Now, imagine an adult child coming to a wealthy parent to say, in effect, "I don't want to wait on you to die to get my share of your estate. Let me have it now, because I want to leave." While that had to be a difficult and painful moment, Jesus told us that the dad did as he was asked and divided up the property between the two sons, allowing the one to essentially cash out his birthright.

With his pockets full of money, the younger son packed a bag and left for a distant country. So, what happened? Did he invest his money or buy a business to become a success and make Dad proud of his decision? No. Verse 13 says, *"[He] squandered his wealth in wild living."* As has always been the case with the world, when the money runs out, the party's over. After the son went completely broke, a famine struck, taking his circumstances from bad to worse. He finally found a job in a man's field feeding pigs, and after a while, as he was literally living in a pigsty, even the pods the swine ate started to look good to him.

But verse 17 starts with an interesting phrase: *"When he came to his senses."* Most of us know exactly what that means—the sudden realization that we've made a huge mistake and massive regret begins to sink in. And then the classic question: *What was I thinking?!* Suddenly, the place the son couldn't wait to leave became the very place where he knew he had to return. His wake-up call made him realize what he had turned his back on and how he had taken his father's care and generosity for granted. He remembered how the hired hands had plenty of food with leftovers to spare. That's when he made the decision to return home. Embarrassed and humbled by his choices, the son planned out his speech to Dad:

> *Father, I have sinned against heaven and against you. I am no longer worthy to be called your son; make me like one of your hired servants.*
> (vv. 18–19)

Imagine the young man's surprise at his father's response:

> *While he was still a long way off, his father saw him and was filled with compassion for him; he ran to his son, threw his arms around him and kissed him.*
> (v. 20)

As he began giving his dad the rehearsed speech, begging for forgiveness and for permission to come back home, the father essentially ignored his plea and called out to the servants:

> *"Quick! Bring the best robe and put it on him. Put a ring on his finger and sandals on his feet. Bring the fattened calf and kill it. Let's have a feast and celebrate. For this son of mine was dead and is alive again; he was lost and is found." So they began to celebrate.*
> (vv. 22–24)

When the older son protested and asked why his father was throwing a huge party for his brother who *"squandered your property with prostitutes"* (v. 30), Jesus ended His story with the dad's response:

> *"My son," the father said, "you are always with me, and everything I have is yours. But we had to celebrate and be glad, because this brother of yours was dead and is alive again; he was lost and is found."*
> (vv. 31–32)

Jesus's point was that the father loved both sons the same, reflecting the unconditional love of our heavenly Father who shows no favoritism. The prodigal's father wasn't angry and judging his wayward son but rather watching and waiting at the end of the road, ready to restore his child from the effects of sin in this fallen world, ready to celebrate his return.

If you are a parent, grandparent, spouse, sibling, or loved one of a prodigal, first, trust that the Father is at work behind the scenes, and, second, pray and hope in faith for the day when you get to experience him or her come home. Through a relationship with Jesus, the heavenly Father is waiting at the end of the road to welcome anyone with open arms to forgive, redeem, and restore.

Reflection

In Jesus's parable about the prodigal, was there anything you realized about your own relationship with God? Explain.

What do you find in Jesus's parable that offers you hope for your prodigal?

Day 2

At the Crossroads

• Music •

Listen to today's song:

"Rescue Story"

• Steve •

Growing up in small-town Arkansas, Jenia and I started going steady when I was in the ninth grade and she was in the eighth. From that year on, we've been a couple. In the home where I grew up, my parents were in one bedroom and my two brothers and I were in the other. Jenia's family owned and ran a gas station, so they lived in a larger, nicer house. I could always count on eating well when I got invited to dinner with her family. While they certainly weren't rich, by comparison to my family, I thought they were. Besides those few differences, Jenia and I had a lot in common and fell in love.

When I was nineteen and she was eighteen, we got married. Overnight, we were "adults" out on our own, no longer under the authority and rules of our churchgoing Christian families. Feeling our independence, we started to spread our wings and see what we might be missing out on in the world.

My grandfather on my mom's side had been a heavy drinker, but later in life he came to Jesus. As a result, my mom wanted nothing to do with the lifestyle that liquor brings. That, along with my grandfather and two uncles being Baptist preachers, meant I grew up in a very strict home. As happens with a lot of kids who are raised in the "thou shalt nots," as soon as I was responsible for my own life, I started to rebel.

Even though I was married, all my high school buddies were still around. Whether Jenia and I met up with friends on the weekend or I went out with the guys, I started drinking. Then, drugs came into the picture and I began to experiment. This direction was obviously not good, especially with a history of addiction in my family. Like Jesus's story of the prodigal, what starts out as just having fun and partying can quickly spin out of control and end in tragedy. Eventually, some of the guys I was hanging out with went to prison or died young.

There came a point where Jenia's raising in a well-respected family kicked in and she started to realize that what began as social drinking for us was turning into substance abuse for me. When I got drunk at home, my wife drew the line. As she tried to talk some sense into me, I wasn't yet willing to grow up, so the stress continued mounting between us until we made the decision to separate.

Thank God, within about six weeks, I reached a crossroads and started realizing the damage I was doing and what I was losing. I had to face up to my addictive DNA and poor choices. Like the prodigal son, I finally came to my senses and knew I had to go back home to set things right. I believe this experience was exactly why I always found grace for Zach through the years when I saw my old life in his. And, of course, also with Crystal, Zach's wife; my daughter, Amy; and my son-in-law, Toby.

To fully commit to Jenia and I getting back together, I knew I had to separate myself from the constant temptations. I realized Jesus had to be at the center of my life and our marriage. I am grateful to God that, once I made that decision, I committed 100 percent and also that I hadn't become addicted to any substance. Jenia had been ready for a change, so we both surrendered our lives to Christ.

Following our new commitment, I discovered what became one of my favorite Bible stories. John 11:21–27 tells us about when Jesus arrived at Lazarus's tomb and the conversation He had with the dead man's sister Martha.

> *"Lord," Martha said to Jesus, "if you had been here,*
> *my brother would not have died. But I know that*
> *even now God will give you whatever you ask."*
> *Jesus said to her, "Your brother will rise again."*
> *Martha answered, "I know he will rise again*
> *in the resurrection at the last day."*

Jesus said to her, "I am the resurrection and the life. The one who believes in me will live, even though they die; and whoever lives by believing in me will never die. Do you believe this?"
"Yes, Lord," she replied, "I believe that you are the Messiah, the Son of God, who is to come into the world."

Like Jenia, me, and Martha in this story, we each have to decide if Jesus is who He says He is. There has to be a point where we each choose whether we will make that same personal confession, *"I believe that you are the Messiah, the Son of God."* There are times when a prodigal leaves behind a family of faith and strays from Christ. Then there are times when, even with a church background, we realize there was never a personal faith at all and the decision for Jesus has to be made for the first time.

We want you to be certain you've answered Jesus's question for yourself: *"Do you believe this?"* If you haven't or need more understanding, go to page 221 in the back of this book for an explanation of the gospel. If you have trusted Christ, then focus today on praying that whatever decision your prodigal needs to make regarding Jesus, God's Spirit will draw him or her to Himself.

Reflection

Was there any part of Steve's testimony or today's Scripture passage that connected to your own life and experience? Explain.

Do you believe that your prodigal has ever made a decision about Jesus? Take a few minutes to write out a prayer for him or her based on your answer.

Day 3

Faith in the Fire, Joy in the Trials

Music

Listen to today's song:

"Old Church Choir"

Jenia

I was raised in Bono, Arkansas, with three brothers, the youngest being ten years older than me. By the time I started school, they had either joined the military or gotten married. Even though Steve said he felt like my family was better off financially than his, that was not my perspective at all. My parents were blue collar too. My father worked for my uncle at his car dealership in Jonesboro until it closed, then Dad purchased one of the three gas stations in town.

Mom worked in my school's cafeteria, eventually becoming the manager and head cook. Our family lived a simple life and our work ethic was always strong. But I will admit that with three older brothers, I was a bit spoiled.

Raised in a loving Christian home and going to the local Methodist church, I believed all the stories about Jesus but never really felt I "knew Him," like I heard others talk about. At around thirteen, feeling somewhat convicted after a sermon, I walked down the aisle. While I don't remember inviting Jesus into my life, they told me I was joining the church.

By the eighth grade, I was a cheerleader who set my sights on a tall, dark, and handsome ninth-grade basketball player named Steve Williams. We dated through high school and then, after graduation, he went off to junior college. I had no idea he had started drinking heavily and was also dabbling in drugs with his buddies. When I was eighteen, after I had been out of high school for a year and was working in a shoe store, we got married. Being honest, our first years together were not pretty, mainly because we started partying every weekend. I never acquired a taste for alcohol and couldn't understand drinking to the point of hanging your head over a toilet. But, being young and figuring this was just what I was supposed to do, I went along with it . . . for a while.

Early in our marriage, our lifestyle brought us to the point where we separated. After about six weeks apart while working to reconcile, we started noticing a big change in the lives of some of our friends who had come to Christ during the popular Jesus Revolution that was sweeping the nation at that time. What we saw happening to them was what we knew we needed. A few of those friends had formed a band playing "Jesus music," and when we went to hear them at Bono Baptist Church, Steve and I were ready. Together, we surrendered our lives to the Lord. (Yes, Christian music played a part in us, as Zach's future parents, coming to Jesus.)

Hungry to learn the Bible, we wanted to be where other brothers and sisters were excited about what God was doing. In that search, we felt like He was calling us to Liberty Bible College in Pensacola, Florida. Moving was a huge step of faith for me because I had only lived in the same small town where I was born. But, in June of 1977, after selling our house in Arkansas, we loaded up a U-Haul and moved to an apartment there, trusting God to provide. About a month in, we gave a sacrificial offering at church for mission work. The next morning, a man knocked on our door and offered Steve a job in the drywall business—exactly what he had been doing at home. That season in Pensacola was one of the best of our lives as we were surrounded by a strong Christian community that became like family.

On June 27, 1978, Zach was born with a very healthy set of lungs. As he shares in his book, *Rescue Story*, we received a prophecy at our church about his life while Zach was being dedicated to the Lord as a baby. About a year later in 1979, after finding out we were expecting again with Amy and that my dad had been diagnosed with cancer, we decided to move back home to Bono. I was thankful that my father was able to get to know his grandkids before he passed away in 1981.

After a couple of years at the family service station, Steve began his drywall business and we were able to build a house near my mother. Because Steve was self-employed, I knew I needed to find a job with insurance, so fifteen years out of high school, I started college to become a nurse and graduated at the top of my class. For the next thirty-plus years, I worked in the nursing field, all the while being a busy wife and mom as the kids were involved in sports and other activities.

When Zach and Amy began to stray from the Lord as teenagers and young adults, Steve and I went through some of the darkest days of our lives. Many times, we picked ourselves up off the floor to press on and trust the Lord. Because we knew His Word is true, we believed His promises, like Paul told us in Romans 10:17:

Consequently, faith comes from hearing the message, and the message is heard through the word about Christ.

The other crucial factor that got us through those prodigal years with our kids was choosing to allow the joy of the Lord to give us His strength and hope. Not happiness, but joy. Happiness depends on circumstances, while joy depends only on God being in our circumstances. In the first chapter of his book, James gave us the foundation for biblical joy:

Consider it pure joy, my brothers and sisters, whenever you face trials of many kinds, because you know that the testing of your faith produces perseverance. Let

perseverance finish its work so that you may be mature and complete, not lacking anything. If any of you lacks wisdom, you should ask God, who gives generously to all without finding fault, and it will be given to you.
(James 1:2–5)

When we search for and learn God's promises throughout the Bible, we have to make the intentional choice to hold on to them by faith. His truth can then bring us joy in trials, help us persevere, and give us wisdom in the journey.

Reflection

Have you ever searched God's Word for His promises? If not, take some time to find one that encourages you. (James 1:2–5 is a good example.) If you have already learned this practice, what is the one verse or passage you go to most for encouragement?

As you are walking through your prodigal's rebellion, ask God to show you how to choose His joy, even when happiness seems elusive. Write out a prayer expressing that to Him now.

Day 4

A Home for Your Heart

Music

Listen to today's song:

"Heart of God"

Steve and Jenia

Here's a big-picture question we want to invite you to thoughtfully answer, being honest with yourself and God. If there were any lyrics in today's song that connected with you, include those.

How do you view God? What is your image or perception of Him?

In today's world, a lot of people seem to have a negative view of God. It's also true that many appear to have no thought of Him at all. Often, at least part of the reason may have something to do with the person's raising by their earthly father (or his absence). Because as parents and children we are flawed and fallen humans, we tend to project the image of our dad onto God. But here's an important truth: Whether you had a great dad, never knew him, or saw him only every other weekend, no father on earth will ever match up to our heavenly Father. So, such a comparison, even in the best-case scenario, can never be accurate. In the Gospel of John alone, Jesus referred to God as Father over one hundred times. His emphasis lets us know that Jesus, as Son and Savior in the Trinity, wants us to understand the heart of our Creator.

For me (Jenia), I've never viewed God as distant and removed, like He's just sitting up there on His throne in heaven. With all His many names and qualities, I see Him *first* as my Father. As a little girl, I remember crawling up in my daddy's lap and how he would give me his undivided attention. My father would listen to me and was always willing to help. That definitely shaped my image of God, and it's still how I see Him today, even years after my earthly father has passed. Like in Zach's song featured today, I see only God's love and open arms, coming from the heart of the original Father. *My* Father.

For me (Steve), even when I was living in disobedience and not headed in the right direction with my faith, I still never saw God as being "out to get me." I've spoken to a lot of people over the years who see Him as angry and vengeful about their sin, but that's simply not true. The reason is because Jesus took "the wrath of God" (His holy response to sin) on Himself on the cross. Romans 5:9 states, *"Since we have now been justified by his blood, how much more shall we be saved from God's wrath through him!"* That's the heart of God and the heart of the gospel—the good news. No matter what your relationship with your dad was (or is), your heavenly Father knows what to do with every single problem and struggle in your life. He literally has *all* the answers. And we can find those in a relationship with Him through Jesus.

In John 14:2–10, Jesus told us about the Father, how His life is available to us, and how we can spend eternity with Him.

> *"My Father's house has many rooms; if that were not so, would I have told you that I am going there to prepare a place for you? And if I go and prepare a place for you, I will come back and take you to be with me that you also may be where I am. You know the way to the place where I am going."*
> *Thomas said to him, "Lord, we don't know where you are going, so how can we know the way?"*
> *Jesus answered, "I am the way and the truth and the life. No one comes to the Father except through me. If*

you really know me, you will know my Father as well.
From now on, you do know him and have seen him."
Philip said, "Lord, show us the Father
and that will be enough for us."
Jesus answered: ". . . Anyone who has seen me has seen the Father. How can you say, 'Show us the Father'? Don't you believe that I am in the Father, and that the Father is in me? The words I say to you I do not speak on my own authority. Rather, it is the Father, living in me, who is doing his work."

Answer these questions for yourself:

- How closely do Jesus's words about God as Father line up with the answer you wrote on the first page today?
- Which do you tend to trust more—Jesus's explanation of God as Father or your own version?
- Do you believe that when you have "seen Jesus" (in the gospels), you have also "seen the Father"?

The most important decision you will ever make has very little to do with the relationship you had or have with your earthly father, whether awesome or awful. The crucial choice is your answer to the question, do you believe Jesus is the way to the Father, the doorway to the heart of God? If you do, you're starting this devotional on the right foundation. If not, the great news is that today can be your day to "come to the Father" through the Son. Or at least start your journey toward Him. (Go to page 221 for more help.)

Reflection

If all you knew about God as Father was what you just read in John 14, how might comparing Him to your earthly father be unfair to all three of you—God, your dad, and yourself?

What spiritual, emotional, or intellectual barriers do you think exist between your prodigal and the heavenly Father? Pray specifically about those today.

Day 5

Carrying the One Back Home

Music

Listen to today's song:

"Lookin' for You"

Steve and Jenia

After we fully surrendered our hearts to Jesus and committed our marriage to Him, we realized the Christian life isn't just a Sunday morning exercise, it's an all day, every day experience in an authentic relationship with the Father through Jesus. Church may be on Sunday morning, but communing with Jesus is 24/7. Christian community can occur anytime we are with brothers and sisters in the Lord. There are days and times of the week where we can meet in a building, but our walk with Christ is a moment-by-moment, day-by-day lifestyle.

As Zach shared in detail in his book, *Rescue Story*, he spent many years running away from the life we had raised him to live, mired in alcohol, drugs, and the rock and roll lifestyle. On a European tour, while in a van going through Spain while his bandmates slept, God answered Zach's desperate prayer to show him He is real by letting him hear Big Daddy Weave's song "Redeemed" on the radio. That night started him down the road of coming home to the Father, which was also miraculously happening back home with Zach's wife, Crystal.

Zach's sister, Amy, went through her own prodigal journey before turning her life around and coming back to the Lord, along with her husband, Toby, one of Zach's high school buddies. So, in our family, we all know the prodigal story well, not just from the Bible but from firsthand experience. We all know exactly what life far away from God is like. But we also understand the reality of coming back home to the Father, experiencing forgiveness, mercy, and, by His grace, the life He offers us each day.

In Luke 15, before Jesus told the parable of the prodigal, He talked about lost sheep. He began this teaching because the Pharisees and teachers of the law, the religious leaders of the day, were condemning and accusing Him of welcoming sinners and eating with them. These men considered themselves to be above engaging and interacting with the people Jesus walked and talked with every day.

Then Jesus told them this parable: "Suppose one of you has a hundred sheep and loses one of them. Doesn't he leave the ninety-nine in the open country and go after the lost sheep until he finds it? And when he finds it, he joyfully puts it on his shoulders and goes home. Then he calls his friends and neighbors together and says, 'Rejoice with me; I have found my lost sheep.' I tell you that in the same way there will be more rejoicing in heaven over one sinner who repents than over ninety-nine righteous persons who do not need to repent." (vv. 3–7)

As a family, we came to see how being a lost sheep is about relation, not location. In fact, this past Sunday, ironically, a lot of church pews had lost sheep sitting in them—those whose hearts are far from the Lord, even though everyone would agree they were in the right location. That's not judgment toward anyone; it's simply the reality of living in a fallen world. It's about the spiritual, not the physical. It's about your heart, not your head. For those reasons, anyone can wander and lose their way.

Our response to life when we're in the valley of failure and disappointment can bring about a rebellion toward God and His ways that, before we know it, can cause us to be far from home. Like Hebrews 2:1 warns, *"We must pay the most careful attention, therefore, to what we have heard, so that we do not drift away."* Yet no matter what causes us to become estranged from God, He goes out to find every sheep and bring them home. Whether someone has been running away from the Father for six weeks or ten years, the good news is as long as they are still breathing, there is always hope and His love is always present. Jesus will leave the ninety-nine to go out, find the one, and bring him or her home. But we must remember that, because He is a loving God, He will not and does not force anyone to go with Him. The ones who are brought home are the ones who agree and allow Him to bring them home.

Reflection

Has there ever been a time in your life when you were closer to God than you are now? Explain.

How might allowing God to help you grow and mature in Him like never before actually help you as you pray your prodigal back home?

Day 6

The Promise in Prayer

Music

Listen to today's song:

"There Was Jesus"

Steve and Jenia

While you are waiting for a prodigal to come home, to return to the Lord for the first time or the last time, prayer should be a crucial, daily part of your journey. But to do that, you have to understand what prayer is and what it isn't. First, praying is simply talking with and listening to God. It's not a formula or script you recite. You are simply sharing your heart as you would with a best friend. Prayer is not about being religious; it's about being in a relationship.

Exodus 33:11 gives us a great example: *"The LORD would speak to Moses face to face, as one speaks to a friend."*

When I (Steve) was walking through those difficult years with Zach, Zach was also working with me. To keep the atmosphere as focused on the Lord as possible, I always played Christian music on the job site. Because hanging drywall and mudding seams is physical, monotonous work, I was able to pray a lot throughout the day. While busy with a tool in my hand, in my mind and spirit I was constantly talking with the Lord.

Because I was always self-employed and writing my own paychecks, our dependence on God was a huge part of our lives. There were seasons when we would be covered up with too much work, praying for the strength to be able to get it all done. Other times we didn't have enough business and had to trust God to meet our needs. Over the years, when we would be slow and constantly praying for provision, something would miraculously come through just in time. That ongoing dependence built a solid foundation so that when we walked through our kids' rebellion, we could pray and believe that God was going to bring them back to Him.

For me (Jenia), during the years when we were raising our family and I was working outside the home, I never had a "prayer closet" and was not enough of a morning person to get up at 5:00 a.m. to pray. That said, anytime I was alone—in the shower, driving to work, or on the way home, whenever I had quiet—I was praying. When Amy started kindergarten and I started college, I was often up after midnight studying. Once my schoolwork was done, alone in the solitude while everyone slept, I would pray. Instead of a set time, I learned to talk to God throughout my day. I believe that's what Paul must have meant when he told us in 1 Thessalonians 5:17 to *"pray continually."* Whether on offense, asking God to work, or defense, praying against the devil, my prayers were constant, taking everything to Jesus. I also spent a lot of time repeating "Thank you, Lord" for His blessings and promises.

Over decades together, whether there was a health issue, financial struggle, or trouble with our kids, we both learned to believe God in prayer. Our faith became like a muscle that just got stronger and stronger over time. We found two principles were helpful and encouraging to us as we talked with God:

1. **Pray specifically**

In Mark 10, as Jesus and the disciples were leaving Jericho, Bartimaeus, who was blind, was sitting by the roadside begging, as he did every day. Hearing that the Lord was nearby, he shouted, *"Jesus, Son of David, have mercy on me!"* (v. 47). The more people tried to get Bartimaeus to be quiet, the louder he yelled. Finally, Jesus stopped and said, *"Call him"* (v. 49). When they told Bartimaeus, he jumped to his feet and made his way to the Lord. Here's where it gets interesting:

"What do you want me to do for you?" Jesus asked him.
The blind man said, "Rabbi, I want to see."

"Go," said Jesus, "your faith has healed you." Immediately he received his sight and followed Jesus along the road. (vv. 51–52)

Now, obviously, Jesus knew the man's need, but what did He ask him? To be specific. Evidently, Jesus didn't want to just hear the generic "have mercy on me." He was after the real need of "I want to see." The takeaway for us about what God wants when we pray is clear. Like the story of Bartimaeus, does He already know your need? Of course He does. But because God wants a relationship with you, He wants to hear your heart, so He asks, *"What do you want me to do for you?"* Be specific.

2. Pray consistently

It's amazing how, no matter how strong we may be, setbacks inside our families can make us feel weak and hopeless. Over the years, there were plenty of times when circumstances would get us down and challenge our faith. During those seasons, we would allow ourselves to feel the emotions, yet we knew we couldn't lie down and stay there. We had to remind ourselves that our hope was not in our circumstances but in Jesus. The question was never, "Do we have hope?" Rather, we reminded ourselves, "*Who* is our hope?" We knew we had to stay focused on the truth of Christ, our living hope. We had to choose to keep praying, even on the tough days when we didn't feel like it.

As you read these verses, focus on the promise made about prayer:

This is the confidence we have in approaching God: that if we ask anything according to his will, he hears us. And if we know that he hears us—whatever we ask—we know that we have what we asked of him.
(1 John 5:14–15)

• Reflection •

What does the story of Bartimaeus and the passage from 1 John 5 say about God's desire for you when you pray?

How can you better apply these two principles—pray specifically and pray consistently—as you intercede for your prodigal?

Day 7

Lining Up with God's Word and Will

Music

Listen to today's song:

"Up There Down Here"

Steve and Jenia

To follow Jesus, we must learn how to line up with God's Word, just as He did. His life and ministry were perfectly in sync with all Scripture that existed up to that time. He did not contradict any detail of any of the books that had been written up to that point. The obedience of His life was proven in how He fulfilled more than three hundred prophecies that had been made about the coming Messiah. So, we need to follow Jesus's example in living by God's promises, precepts, and principles, and His Word should be a vital part of our prayer life as well. Our requests to God should be aligned with the truths in the Bible. A simple way to remember this is by a *do* and a *don't.*

- **Do** ask for what He has promised and taught us in His Word.

  We can speak God's Word back to Him in faith. Praying according to His Word helps us live according to His will. God will always honor His Word. When we read and know the Scriptures, we'll be much less likely to desire something that goes against His Word and therefore against His will.

- **Don't** ask for anything that isn't lined up with His Word.

  Sometimes we can be tempted to beg or bargain with God to act on our behalf, but we are actually asking out of selfish or immature motives. We want our own will and are not concerned with Him or the welfare of others. We must remember that because God is just and righteous, He will never compromise His Word. Bottom line—no one gets to be the exception to the rule, so we shouldn't ask for or expect that.

Here's an example of praying according to His Word by relying on what we have already been told in the Bible. There are two passages in Matthew where Jesus taught us how to handle conflict resolution and pursue reconciliation in relationships. In 5:23–24, He told us what to do when we have offended someone:

> *Therefore, if you are offering your gift at the altar and there remember that your brother or sister has something against you, leave your gift there in front of the altar. First go and be reconciled to them; then come and offer your gift.*

Jesus clearly said that keeping our personal relationships right is important to God. He expects us to correct those *before* we come to Him. He wants our horizontal relationships to be in right standing so we may come to our vertical relationship with Him also in right standing. Later, in Matthew 18:15–17, He told us what to do if we are the offended party.

> *If your brother or sister sins, go and point out their fault, just between the two of you. If they listen to you, you have won them over. But if they will not listen, take one or two others along, so that "every matter may be established by the testimony of two or three witnesses." If they still refuse to listen, tell it to the church; and if they refuse to listen even to the church, treat them as you would a pagan or a tax collector.*

So, if we know we have offended someone and choose to ignore or justify our actions, how effective should we think our prayers will be? If we're at church and ask people to pray for someone who has offended us before we have gone to talk to the person, how do we suppose God feels about getting His instructions out of order? But what about if we do everything Jesus asked of us and the person won't forgive or refuses to acknowledge his or her part? Paul covered that situation in Romans 12:18: *"If it is possible, as far as it depends on you, live at peace with everyone."* God won't hold you responsible for someone else's actions. He only asks you to take care of your part to "live at peace."

Second Timothy 3:16–17 offers us a powerful description of God's Word and what it is capable of accomplishing in our lives.

> *All Scripture is God-breathed and is useful for teaching, rebuking, correcting and training in righteousness, so that the servant of God may be thoroughly equipped for every good work.*

We hope today you have seen how vital God's Word is to the way you live your life and how you pray. As you walk through the journey with your prodigal and deepen in your walk with Jesus, keep these truths about His Word in mind when you pray. You will be able to experience every promise that God has for you and your loved one.

Reflection

Did either of the two passages of Jesus's teaching in Matthew prompt you toward any action you need to take in a relationship? Explain.

How can you apply the "do" from today (*Do* ask for what He has promised and taught us in His Word) in your prayer life for your prodigal?

Day 8

Praying God's Word

Music

Listen to today's song:

"Heaven Help Me"

Steve and Jenia

Yesterday we talked about the importance of aligning our lives with God's Word. Another important spiritual discipline we learned many years ago was the power of combining God's Word into our prayer life, both when we prayed together as a couple and when praying alone. Because consistent and targeted prayer is so crucial as you walk through the prodigal season with your loved one, we want to show you exactly how this works and also give you some of the passages we prayed that were effective in our family.

Feel free to read from whatever translation you choose. If you are new to Bible reading, you can go to Bible-Gateway.com and look through all the available versions to find one that works best for you. If you've been reading the Bible for many years like we have, sometimes it's good to switch things up and read a different translation for a while to give yourself a fresh perspective on Scripture. The most important thing is that you understand and connect with the words you are reading and praying.

For me (Jenia), I often prayed Paul's words in Ephesians 3:14–19. As you read the passage, think of this as a prayer for your prodigal.

For this reason I kneel before the Father, from whom every family in heaven and on earth derives its name. I pray that out of his glorious riches he may strengthen you with power through his Spirit in your inner being, so that Christ may dwell in your hearts through faith. And I pray that you, being rooted and established in love, may have power, together with all the Lord's holy people, to grasp how wide and long and high and deep is the love of Christ, and to know this love that surpasses knowledge—that you may be filled to the measure of all the fullness of God.

Many psalms are actually prayers or about prayer. They're often written in the first person, so you can read them as is, making King David's words your own. That's likely one of the reasons that chapters like Psalm 23 have become universal in so many settings. *"The LORD is my shepherd, I lack nothing"* (v. 1) takes on the perspective of the person reading or speaking. In Matthew 6, Jesus gave His disciples what became known as the Lord's Prayer, and anyone today can read or say these words exactly as Jesus did, making them their own. Being in a group of people who recite His prayer together is always a powerful moment.

We know there are going to be plenty of days when you feel discouraged and hopeless. At times you may not be sure what to pray or how to pick yourself back up and find the encouragement to move forward. When that happens, David's honest, often blunt psalms can be very helpful. As early as Psalm 6, we can see his very distraught and desperate cries to God:

All night long I flood my bed with weeping
and drench my couch with tears.
My eyes grow weak with sorrow;
they fail because of all my foes.
Away from me, all you who do evil,
for the LORD has heard my weeping.
The LORD has heard my cry for mercy;
the LORD accepts my prayer.
(vv. 6–9)

Obviously David was in a lot of emotional pain and knew God was his only possible source of help. Have you ever felt this way? Can you relate to those feelings? We must remember this is God's Word that He ordained to be written and given to us. Therefore, every single word has a purpose. God was showing us how David's words were acceptable to Him and that they are acceptable for us to pray as well. In Psalm 13, David began with expressing his sorrow, but then his faith became apparent.

How long, LORD? Will you forget me forever?
How long will you hide your face from me?
How long must I wrestle with my thoughts
and day after day have sorrow in my heart?
How long will my enemy triumph over me?
(vv. 1–2)

It's hard for most of us to imagine asking God questions like these. But there are a number of places in Psalms where David asked "How long, LORD?" whether he was waiting for an answer or watching evil appear to triumph or both. But look at what he said a few verses later:

But I trust in your unfailing love;
my heart rejoices in your salvation.
I will sing the LORD's praise,
for he has been good to me.
(vv. 5–6)

In Psalm 119, the longest chapter in the Bible, we find some incredible, faith-filled prayers. Here's a great example:

Teach me, LORD, the way of your decrees,
that I may follow it to the end.
Give me understanding, so that I may keep your law

and obey it with all my heart.
Direct me in the path of your commands,
for there I find delight.
Turn my heart toward your statutes
and not toward selfish gain.
Turn my eyes away from worthless things;
preserve my life according to your word.
(vv. 33–37)

Whether we are reading David's prayers in Psalms, Jesus's teaching in the Gospels, or Paul's instruction in his letters, their words can become our prayers for what we desire to see God accomplish in our lives. As you read God's Word, watch for verses that you can pray. Take some time to go through Psalms and mark some passages that speak to you and connect with your own heart, then pray those words back to God.

Reflection

How might using Scripture, like the prayers found in Psalms, influence and improve your prayer life?

Try praying Ephesians 3:14–19 for your prodigal, just as I (Jenia) did for our kids.

Day 9

Personalizing the Word in Your Prayers

Music

Listen to today's song:

"I Got You"

Steve and Jenia

Yesterday we talked about how to pray God's Word. Another way to use Scripture passages as specific and targeted prayers for your loved one or yourself is to personalize them. The point of this practice is not to alter or abuse the words or their meaning but simply to create a proactive prayer by replacing the pronouns with someone's name or your own. Yesterday I (Jenia) shared with you about praying Ephesians 3:14–19. When I was praying for Zach, this is how I would personalize verses 16–19. The bracketed words mark the changes.

God, I pray that out of [Your] glorious riches [You] may strengthen [Zach] with power through [Your] Spirit in [his] inner being, so that [You] may dwell in [his heart] through faith. And I pray that [Zach], being rooted and established in love, may have power, together with all the Lord's people, to grasp how wide and long and high and deep is [Your love], and to know this love that surpasses knowledge—that [Zach] may be filled to the measure of all [Your] fullness.

You can see how a few simple changes make this powerful passage into a very personal and impactful prayer. When you're struggling and need to pray this for yourself, here's what that could look like:

God, I pray that out of [Your] glorious riches [You] may strengthen [me] with power through [Your] Spirit in [my] inner being, so that [You] may dwell in [my heart] through faith. And I pray that [I], being rooted and established in love, may have power, together with all the Lord's people, to grasp how wide and long and high and deep is [Your love], and to know this love that surpasses knowledge—that [I] may be filled to the measure of all [Your] fullness.

Again, to be clear, this approach is not advocating that anyone rewrite or change the meaning of the Bible; it's simply interchanging the necessary pronouns to personalize the Word for praying specifically as we talked about in Day 6.

Below is an example that we have also prayed often—Proverbs 4:20–23. Let's begin with the actual passage.

My son, pay attention to what I say;
turn your ear to my words.
Do not let them out of your sight,
keep them within your heart;
for they are life to those who find them
and health to one's whole body.
Above all else, guard your heart,
for everything you do flows from it.

Now, the personal version with the words from Scripture italicized:

"Lord, I pray that I will *pay attention to what* You *say* and *turn* my *ear to* Your *words.* I pray that I would *not let them out of* my *sight* and would *keep them within* my *heart.* I thank You, Lord, that *they are life and health to* me. I pray, *above all else,* that I will *guard* my *heart, for everything* I *do flows from it.* I praise You and thank You in Jesus's name, amen."

Now, the prodigal version:

"Lord, I pray that ____________ will *pay attention to what* You *say* and *turn* his/her *ear* to Your *words.* I pray that __________ would *not let them out of* his/her *sight* and would *keep them within* his/her *heart.* I thank You, Lord, that *they are life and health to* __________. I pray,

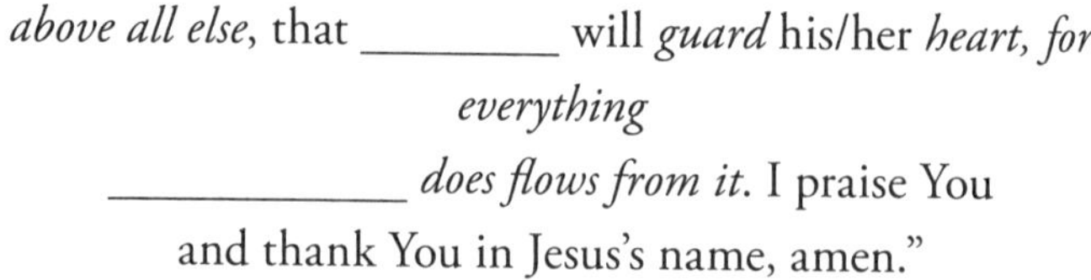

above all else, that ________ will *guard* his/her *heart, for everything* ____________ *does flows from it.* I praise You and thank You in Jesus's name, amen."

While this gives you one example of how to adapt a Scripture passage to both personal and prodigal prayers, hopefully you see how you can adapt many other verses in this way as you pray. Especially once you know a Bible passage really well, you'll get to the point where reading as a prayer will become second nature.

The entire chapter of John 17 gives us an incredibly powerful and personal prayer that Jesus lifted to the Father just before His arrest. In the final section, His words are for all His followers, even those to come, including us. Here are verses 24–26:

Father, I want those you have given me to be with me where I am, and to see my glory, the glory you have given me because you loved me before the creation of the world. Righteous Father, though the world does not know you, I know you, and they know that you have sent me. I have made you known to them, and will continue to make you known in order that the love you have for me may be in them and that I myself may be in them.

Being able to read Jesus's very intimate prayer to the Father about what He had accomplished and what He was about to complete for us all is such an incredible privilege. As we read His words, we know the nature of the prodigal journey is about the Enemy working hard to separate and divide heavenly and earthly relationships. Reminding ourselves of Jesus's will and desire for unity and multiplication on earth as it is in heaven can be a great encouragement for us.

Over the past three days, we have covered the crucial discipline of engaging with and living out the Word of God in our lives. We hope and pray you will adopt these disciplines so that you may experience the unique power of how the Word and the Spirit work together to transform you and touch those you pray for.

Reflection

Today, place your name in one of the above passages and pray for yourself.

Place your prodigal's name in one of the above passages and pray for him or her today.

Day 10

It's Not How You Start, It's How You End

Music

Listen to today's song:

"Revival"

Zach

If you have heard me share my testimony at one of my concerts or read my book, *Rescue Story*, you know that from high school to college and into my adult life, I was chasing the world. I had bought into the lie that I had to live a certain way to achieve what I wanted, in basketball and then later with music. I thought if you play rock and roll, you have to live the lifestyle. I grew increasingly reckless over the years as drugs and alcohol became an everyday part of my life. While I was never addicted, I was definitely using it all as medication to numb myself, trying to fend off all the toxicity I was feeling and fill the huge void in my heart.

As you've heard from my parents, I grew up in a Christian home, and we were in church every time the doors were open. I believed in God, but later after I had amassed a laundry list of sins, I questioned if He could still love me and forgive me for all the things I had done and was still doing. When my parents would come see me play in those smoky bars, the entire time they were silently praying that one day my life would be surrendered for God's glory.

Year after year, through the mess that I'd been living for far too long, my mom and dad continued to show me love. They were trusting God and believing that His plans would someday unfold for me. Now, living life on the other side, I can see how so often we all want to pray and expect God to do something right away. We want Him to move on our timetable. But that's just not how it works. That's not how He works. Are there times when God does a miracle in the moment? Yes. But for the majority of us, it takes time. He won't and doesn't force anyone to surrender, and because we are ruled by our sin nature, turning things around can be a journey. At least that's how it was for me.

Yet I can clearly look back and see now that even though I was running as fast and as far as I could, God was pursuing me. Coming out of that experience, I realized there are two common lies that many people believe about Him. The first is this: "I have to get my act together before I can come to God." Picture this situation: A guy tells his friend, "I had an accident and can't drive my car." The friend asks,

"So, is it in the body shop?" He answers, "Oh no, it's way too messed up. I would be so embarrassed to face those people once they see how bad the damage is." The friend asks, "What?! So, what are you going to do?" He answers, "I'm just going to keep the car in the garage and try to fix it myself. I don't have the right tools and don't know what to do, but maybe once I get it in better shape, I can take it to the shop." Ridiculous, right? But that's exactly what we're saying when we think we have to "fix ourselves first" or "get our act together" before handing over our mess to God.

When I came to Christ, I gave Him all my brokenness. He already saw it all and knew what was there, even better than I did. Part of the reason the gospel is called the good news is because He knows exactly what to do with us. Romans 5:8 says it all:

> *But God demonstrates his own love for us in this:*
> *While we were still sinners, Christ died for us.*

Now, here's the second lie: "Once I come to Him, He's going to make my life perfect. All my troubles will be over." Well, I can tell you from firsthand experience that, while I felt His love, peace, and grace right away, I became nowhere close to perfect and am still not today. That's why the Christian life is a transformation. Not an event, a one-and-done, but a journey. It's a marathon, not a sprint. After years of knowing Jesus, the apostle Paul set the record straight when he shared,

Brothers and sisters, I do not consider myself yet to have taken hold of it. But one thing I do: Forgetting what is behind and straining toward what is ahead, I press on toward the goal to win the prize for which God has called me heavenward in Christ Jesus.
(Philippians 3:13–14)

When I gave my life to the Lord, I simply said, "I don't want to be who I am anymore. I'm honestly crying out for Your help. God, I'm sick of this and I can't do it on my own." In that moment, He took over. For anyone, especially prodigals, life is not about how you start, it's about how you end. I gave you two common lies today, but here's a truth to end on: I can tell you that my worst days today with Jesus are so much better than my best days when I was living without Him. Because God can take the messiest parts of our lives and turn them into a message.

Reflection

Have you ever struggled with the two lies I (Zach) talked about today? Explain.

How does my (Zach's) story give you encouragement and more understanding of how to pray for your prodigal?

Day 11

A Father Who Is Always There

Music

Listen to today's song:

"Survivor"

Crystal

For starters, I grew up the opposite of Zach. At a young age, my life became hard. You hear a lot of people these days say their families are dysfunctional, but the best way I know how to describe my growing up was I didn't feel any love in our house. My parents did consider themselves to be spiritual, but not Christian. God, and especially Jesus, were never talked about. But when I was ten years old, I became curious about the Baptist church at the end of our street. Searching for some sort of connection and hope, I started walking there on Sunday mornings by myself. After meeting the pastor and getting to know a few of the kids my age, they invited me to go with them to a Billy Graham revival.

I remember sitting there hearing the gospel for the first time. At the altar call, as I watched all the people get up and walk forward, I was feeling a lot of powerful emotions and got down on my knees. I had no idea what all of this meant, but I knew something just felt right. I wanted in on whatever was taking place there and to know more about this Jesus that Billy Graham was talking about. I wish I could tell you that I came to Christ that night and lived happily ever after. Unfortunately, as often happens when a kid from a non-Christian home begins to get close to faith, the Enemy started working overtime to put a stop to any change. Not long after that first experience with Jesus, life in our family went from bad to worse and I was introduced to drugs for the first time. From there, I began to drift farther away from what happened at the revival.

In my early adult life, I started calling myself an atheist, more out of a lack of belief in anything than trying to prove that God doesn't exist. When I went to college, I decided to minor in biblical studies, thinking that if I knew more, I could better prove Scripture wrong. But, looking back, it's interesting that I wanted to know more about something I was trying so hard to convince myself wasn't true.

By the time I was a single mom with two kids and met Zach, I had honestly just stopped caring about faith or belief of any kind. Yet, deep down, the truth was that my spirit and my heart were broken by life and my own choices. As Zach and I were constantly partying and he was playing in the band, I became more and more dissatisfied with what I saw as a pointless, empty life. Walking into a bar and dealing with all the noise and drunkenness, I could see those people were slowly dying. I knew there had to be more than this, even though everyone was working so hard to prove they were living their best life while ordering another round. I didn't understand it yet, but that was God working on my heart and changing my mind. Increasingly in that season, I was more than ready for something different for our family.

When Zach came home from the road and told me he wanted us to go to church with one of his bandmates and his wife, I was surprised but also up for the challenge. On that first Sunday morning, we both could feel there was something to this. We were on the same page in our search for truth. But, as we talked about in detail in the book *Rescue Story*, Zach wasn't done yet. Not until that night on the tour in Europe. While Zach was away, dealing with his own heart, God was speaking to me. I began to think a lot about the forgiveness and grace that Zach's parents had shown him. While I didn't understand it, I knew their love was because of their relationship with Jesus.

Finally, one day, feeling a lot of different emotions, I started praying out loud. That's when I heard God's voice speak to my spirit, "Crystal, I'm here for you. I've always been with you. I've always been your Father. When no one else was there for you, I was." That was my "come to Jesus moment." I soon found out that it was very close to the same time God was speaking to Zach on the other side of the world. From there, as I began to receive His love and grace for the first time, God began to work on both our hearts and lives. We had no idea how He was about to radically change everything, but that's exactly what Jesus will do when we surrender our lives to Him.

All this is for your benefit, so that the grace that is reaching more and more people may cause thanksgiving to overflow to the glory of God. Therefore we do not lose heart. Though outwardly we are wasting away, yet inwardly we are being renewed day by day. For our light and momentary troubles are achieving for us an eternal glory that far outweighs them all. So we fix our eyes not on what is seen, but on what is unseen, since what is seen is temporary, but what is unseen is eternal.
(2 Corinthians 4:15–18)

Reflection

Has a difficult life circumstance or temptation ever distracted or disrupted your walk with Jesus? Explain.

Do you know if any circumstance has derailed your prodigal's faith and is being used as spiritual leverage by the Enemy to keep him or her away from God? If so, write that down and then use those thoughts in your prayer today.

Day 12

Freedom Is a Choice

Music

Listen to today's song:

"Chain Breaker"

Steve and Jenia

With Zach growing up in Bono, Arkansas, the same town where we had grown up, he struggled with what a lot of kids in small-town USA face. With not much to do, he and his buddies got bored quickly, so they often gave in to temptation. Early on, it was getting caught smoking behind the shed or stealing candy from the local convenience store, but the seeds of rebellion were planted and growing.

At the same time that Zach began playing basketball and getting really good, he began smoking cigarettes with the neighborhood buddies, which later turned into marijuana with his teammates. Then alcohol entered the picture. Darkness was whispering in his ear and tempting him to walk further away from the truth he knew. Peer pressure, which Zach was guilty of creating just as much as the others, was leading all those boys down the wrong road.

By Zach's senior year in high school, their team was considered the favorite to win state, and scholarship offers were coming in to play college basketball. One night in the high school parking lot, several of the guys on the team were sitting in a car when someone got out a joint, lit it up, and all the guys took part. In a small town, word got out about the incident, and the next day they were all called into the principal's office with the basketball coach and the sheriff there. Unfortunately, Zach and two of his teammates took the fall. We will never forget the night we had to go to a school board meeting with an attorney. After Zach was suspended and kicked off the basketball team, he felt like his dream was over. That's when he made the decision to quit school and get his GED.

His feelings of shame, embarrassment, and failure became chains that wrapped him up so tight he could no longer see the truth that God still had a plan for his life, that God still loved him the same, that his life was valuable and everything could work out in time. From there, the downward spiral began. Slowly at first, but as the years passed, the speed increased.

As his parents, we knew Zach was raised on God's Word and that His truth was still in his spirit. Was it covered up? Yes. But was it still there in his heart? Yes. That helped us hold on to God's promises as we began a decade of praying for Zach's eyes to be opened and his heart to be able to hear from God. When we would go to the bars to hear Zach and the band play one of his original songs, we always heard the overtones of what he knew from the Word in his lyrics. Of course, we had no idea that years later, the world would hear God's Word in all his songs!

In John 8, when Jesus was speaking on the Mount of Olives, some Jews who were listening heard Him say, *"If you hold to my teaching, you are really my disciples. Then you will know the truth, and the truth will set you free"* (vv. 31–32). As often happened, they were confused by Jesus's words, specifically "set you free."

> *They answered him, "We are Abraham's descendants and have never been slaves of anyone. How can you say that we shall be set free?"*
> (v. 33)

Jesus knew that many of the ones gathered were actually looking for a way to get rid of Him. He knew their hearts were not to follow Him, but to finish Him.

> *Jesus replied, "Very truly I tell you, everyone who sins is a slave to sin. Now a slave has no permanent place in the family, but a son belongs to it forever. So if the Son sets you free, you will be free indeed."*
> (vv. 34–36)

Jesus's point was that, because of the sin nature in us all, we are bound up with the chains of rebellion. From addiction to anger, from judgment to jealousy, from lust to lying, we are all guilty of sins others can see and some they will never see. Regardless, the only Source of freedom is the Son of God. The only way to go from being a slave to sin to a son or daughter of the Savior is through surrender to Christ. The only way the chains of sin can be broken is by the Chain Breaker—Jesus.

When anyone hits their knees and calls out to Him to save them, the chains of sin are broken. Can we choose to keep them wrapped around us? Yes. Can we decide later to become bound again? Yes. But God gives each of us free will to make the daily choice to say no to any chain. And nothing is too strong or too powerful for Jesus.

Always remember, when you are struggling or watching someone you love battle their own chains, Jesus is the Chain Breaker. We can trust His promises. We speak from first-hand experience when we say to not give up on believing and placing your faith in God, because He will never give up on anyone, no matter how far away they've run or how many chains bind them.

Reflection

What were, or what are, your chains? What chains has Jesus broken in your life? Explain.

What are the chains you feel are wrapped around your prodigal that you need to ask Jesus to break? Once you have listed those, start praying against those chains today.

Day 13

The One Who Never Gives Up

Music

Listen to today's song:

"Middle of a Miracle"

Steve and Jenia

For any parent committed to following Christ and doing his or her best to live by the truth of God's Word, it is always a painful experience when our kids choose not to follow in our footsteps of faith. Because we had walked through a season of living the prodigal life ourselves, we wanted so much more for Zach and Amy. We desperately wanted them to not have to "learn the hard way" like we did. It was so hard for us to watch as they both strayed in their choices because we loved them so much. The very fact that nothing our kids could ever do would make us stop loving them is also what makes it so tough for us as parents to persevere when our hearts are broken.

Back in the days of Zach's rebellion, after he and Crystal had started living together, they asked to come over to talk with us. Sitting in our living room, they told us they were going to have a baby. Knowing their lifestyle and that they were not married at the time made their news very bittersweet for us. Not long after that, Amy and her boyfriend, Toby, who were also living together, came over. In an almost exact repeat of Zach and Crystal's visit, they told us they were expecting too.

That was hard news for us to accept—twice. Now, of course we wanted grandchildren. Of course we wanted to experience our kids having their own kids. No question about that at all. And we were going to unconditionally love those grandbabies, no matter what. Our feelings were not about judgment or condemnation of anyone; we simply wanted God's best for our family.

Putting our personal feelings aside, we just kept loving them all, praying and hoping. Being honest, we asked God a lot of questions like, "Lord, where did we mess up?! Where in the world did we go wrong as parents? Why would our kids completely reject our faith and the life we worked so hard to live in front of them?" We never questioned God, just ourselves.

That was the bad news in those painful days. Now, here's the good news. Eventually, God moved in miraculous ways to radically change the lives of all four of them. You've heard from Zach and Crystal. For Amy and Toby, about five years after they got married, Amy realized the severity of Toby's addiction. By that point, they had two children. Much like Jenia had done with me (Steve), Amy decided she didn't want to live any longer the way they had been. She came to the conclusion that she didn't want to raise her kids like that. One day she told Toby, "You either get help or we're done."

Agreeing with her, they drove to a rehab facility and he checked in. That was the crossroads that began their life change. They committed their lives to Jesus and, today, through that organization, John 3:16 Ministries, Toby volunteers there to help men find the same freedom he found. He has been clean for many years and now helps other men find the same freedom he found.

Had you told us back then—after both our kids had come to us with their news of being pregnant while living the lifestyles they were—that both couples' stories would turn out the way they did, we would have had a tough time believing how something so miraculous could happen. But, friend, that is the difference that Jesus Christ can make when we invite Him into our story. While there are certainly no guarantees in this life, He is the One who can turn *anyone* around.

The Bible is filled with rescue stories, much like what happened in our family. We see time and time again how a hopeless situation was restored and redeemed for God's glory. One of the best examples is the disciple Peter. In most Bibles, the subheading at Luke 22 reads, "Peter Disowns Jesus." It's interesting that when we are at our worst, we can believe that Jesus will disown us when, most often, that is actually the choice *we* make. In this story, after walking with the Messiah so closely every day for three years, when the threat of arrest and an angry mob came, Peter denied any connection to Jesus not once but three times. Afterward, verse 62 states, *"And [Peter] went outside and wept bitterly."*

If we flip over to Acts 2, we read about a guy who stood up and preached about Jesus to a crowd of thousands with amazing authority. Verse 41 says, *"Those who accepted his message were baptized, and about three thousand were added to their number that day."* The man in Luke 22 and Acts 2 were one and the same—Peter. So, what in the world happened to transform him?

The answer is found in John 21, which recounts a conversation between Peter and the resurrected Jesus.

> *When they had finished eating, Jesus said to Simon Peter,*
> *"Simon son of John, do you love me more than these?"*
> *"Yes, Lord," he said, "you know that I love you."*
> *Jesus said, "Feed my lambs."*
> *Again Jesus said, "Simon son of John, do you love me?"*
> *He answered, "Yes, Lord, you know that I love you."*
> *Jesus said, "Take care of my sheep."*
> *The third time he said to him, "Simon son of John, do you love me?"*
> *Peter was hurt because Jesus asked him the third time, "Do you love me?" He said, "Lord, you know all things; you know that I love you."*
> *Jesus said, "Feed my sheep." . . . Then he said to him, "Follow me!"*
> (vv. 15–17, 19)

Jesus didn't condemn or disown Peter for his choices on the night of the trial. Instead, He sought him out, rescued him, and restored him. On the other side of that moment on the beach, Peter was a new person with a new mission. That is exactly what God desires for us all. The gospel is indeed for everyone. We are so grateful our family can now be a testimony to that truth. You can believe the same transformation is possible for your prodigal.

Reflection

How can our family's story encourage you when you feel helpless and hopeless about the prodigal you love and want to see come home to the Lord?

What are some ways that Peter's story—from his denial of Jesus at His trial, to their conversation on the beach, to the sermon in Acts—gives you hope for your prodigal?

Day 14

The Author of Truth vs. the Father of Lies

Music

Listen to today's song:

"Fear Is a Liar"

Steve and Jenia

Because of our sin nature, we all struggle with feelings of insecurity on some level. Even someone who acts arrogant and cocky is simply covering up and overcompensating for feelings of inadequacy. Some insecurities we may grow out of or overcome, while others can stay with us for a lifetime. The feeling of "I am not enough" plagues us all somehow, somewhere in our lives. You can even hear this in interviews with highly successful people as they talk about dealing with this same struggle. We might look at their lives and not be able to understand why or how they could possibly feel that way. But that's just proof that everyone battles this terrible monster called fear.

As Zach's parents, we saw how many of his struggles, up until he surrendered to Jesus, were because of the fear of not being enough. I (Jenia) don't think either of us really understood how deeply those feelings were entrenched in his heart. Especially in his senior year, he struggled with thinking he had let down his basketball team, his friends, and us. Then, add the feeling of letting himself down—the one person he could never escape. After a while, those pressures and insecurities created a vicious cycle for Zach.

Even after he gave his life to Jesus and signed his record deal, I (Steve) remember Zach telling Crystal and us about being out on tour, opening for a headline artist, walking out on stage with his acoustic guitar, and feeling like he wasn't good enough to be a voice for Jesus. Zach's chains were broken, but healing doesn't happen overnight. Some healing takes time. Some deep-seated struggles are going to stick around and fight us. In fact, some battles can intensify when we start trying to live a life of obedience to God. The Enemy doesn't like losing his grip on anyone, so he can keep throwing the same old darts to try and derail us. When he knows he no longer has our souls, he will work overtime to keep us from being all God wants us to be.

The apostle Paul, while in prison because of his stand for the gospel, wrote these words to his young disciple Timothy, which is great counsel that also applies to us:

For God has not given us a spirit of fear and timidity, but of power, love, and self-discipline. So never be ashamed to tell others about our Lord. And don't be ashamed of me, either, even though I'm in prison for him. With the strength God gives you, be ready to suffer with me for the sake of the Good News. For God saved us and called us to live a holy life. He did this, not because we deserved it, but because that was his plan from before the beginning of time—to show us his grace through Christ Jesus. And now he has made all of this plain to us by the appearing of Christ Jesus, our Savior. He broke the power of death and illuminated the way to life and immortality through the Good News.
(2 Timothy 1:7–10 NLT)

When we feel insecure, unworthy, and fearful, God offers us His power, love, and self-discipline. When we as Christians are afraid to do something we know we need to do, when we push through and apply discipline to a situation, when we don't give up but just keep putting ourselves out there, God can use that faith and belief to give us strength to keep trying, to keep on keeping on, bringing confidence and security to our minds and hearts.

What if on that very first tour Zach would have quit? What if he had told his record label and his team, "I can't do this. I can't overcome these feelings of fear I'm having on the stage. I'm out"? The answer honestly has very little to do with Zach and everything to do with the millions of people who would have never heard the gospel through his music. Our decision to allow God to help us overcome our own fears and insecurities affects not only us but, ultimately, anyone we could reach for His glory. The devil wants to harm us, but his real goal is to try and keep us from reaching people for Christ.

In John 8:44, Jesus taught about Satan,

> *"He has always hated the truth, because there is no truth in him. When he lies, it is consistent with his character; for he is a liar and the father of lies"* (NLT).

Please know this: If you have trusted Jesus and placed your life into His hands, then the voice that keeps saying you aren't good enough, that you can never be anything, or that you can't overcome your struggles or defeat your fears, that is your enemy, and he is not telling you the truth. He is lying to you. You have to listen to Jesus, the Author of all truth.

When the Enemy tells you to give up praying for your prodigal, that he or she is too far gone, or that God isn't listening or doesn't care, remind the devil that he is a liar. Stand on God's truth and pray in faith to defeat the fear.

Reflection

What fear do you continue to struggle with that is holding you back in your life? Explain.

What fear or lie has the Enemy been whispering in your ear about your prodigal? Be specific in your answer and then pray through what you write down.

Day 15

Less Is More

Music

Listen to today's song:

"Less like Me"

Steve

As parents who follow Christ, the life lessons we are to teach our kids should come through the filter of God and His Word. With that, here are a few things I want to share that I have learned over the years. This concept is demonstrated early in Scripture as we can see in Deuteronomy 6:6–9.

These commandments that I give you today are to be on your hearts. Impress them on your children. Talk about them when you sit at home and when you walk along the road, when you lie down and when you get up. Tie them as symbols on your hands and bind them on your foreheads. Write them on the doorframes of your houses and on your gates.

God's people were encouraged to teach their children the ways of the Lord. When? On Sunday mornings and Wednesday nights? Well, yes, but also at home, out in the world, first thing when they got up, and last thing before they lay down at night. The spirit of this passage is that God is an integral and constant aspect of the Christian family's life. There is no separation between the sacred and the secular. He is involved and intertwined in every detail of their days. That brings us to the first truth.

1. Teach, don't preach.

While, of course, our words are important to share, there is another powerful teacher—our actions. There's an old saying, "I can't hear what you're saying because your life is too loud." We should want to help others believe the gospel, not make it more difficult for them to believe. Often, God uses our actions to sow God's Word into others' lives. Especially today, a life that is lived out unashamedly and unapologetically for Jesus can turn a good sermon into the best we could ever preach. This is the point that Paul made in his book to Titus. The lives of Christians should "make the teaching about God our Savior attractive in every way" (Titus 2:10 NLT).

2. Be the exception, not the rule.

As we've talked about, for many years Zach worked with me in the drywall business. It's common knowledge that a lot of folks who work in construction have developed a bad reputation. Sadly, for a long time, alcohol and drug use have been prevalent among contractors who work on homes. Over the years, I've been unfairly lumped in with some bad actors in the business. There are even shady people who will use Christian phrases and symbols in their business to try and create a false sense of integrity and honor. That practice has caused a lot of harm to the Christian witness. Knowing that this made my words cheap to many people, I always worked extra hard to set an example and be the exception in my business. I tried to treat my employees and my clients with respect. Zach and I have talked about how he picked up on those unspoken lessons and how they had an impact on him.

Let my teaching fall like rain
and my words descend like dew,
like showers on new grass,
like abundant rain on tender plants.
(Deuteronomy 32:2)

3. Use more of God's Word, less of yours.

Over the years, after getting some age and wisdom on me, I have seen how worthless our words can be. We can become just more noise to people, another voice in the crowd trying to get attention to be heard. But when we either quote God's Word or speak the truths found in Scripture, those have a power like no other force in this world.

So is my word that goes out from my mouth:
It will not return to me empty,
but will accomplish what I desire
and achieve the purpose for which I sent it.
(Isaiah 55:11)

When we speak God's Word, when His truth leaves our mouths, He promises it will go out and accomplish His purposes. Not returning as empty, but filled. Not worthless, but worthy. Not stagnant, but strong. Even if the person we are speaking with doesn't know he or she has heard Scripture, God can work in and through His Word to produce whatever He wants in that person's heart. The truth can hit someone's ears, enter into their spirits, and change their minds. I believe these three bits of counsel are vitally important when we have prodigal children of any age. But in our culture today, it's always a valid way to live out our faith.

Reflection

Which of the three points spoke most to your life? Explain.

In your relationship with your prodigal, which one of these might help make the most difference? Explain.

Day 16

Foundations and Floods

• Music •

Listen to today's song:

"Friend in High Places"

• Steve and Jenia •

Being in the construction business for most of my (Steve's) working life, and having Zach work with me for years, we know a thing or two about building a home from the ground up, from the shovel to the shingles. The most crucial part is the foundation—the base the house sits on determines its strength. If a home that costs millions of dollars is constructed on the wrong footing, eventually, cracks will begin to show up in the walls, doors will stick and not open or close, and, in the worst situations, part of the house can actually break away and separate. The unseen foundation affects the entire home. But another problem can occur, even when a house is built on a strong slab. If the ground below starts to move due to water, erosion, or fissures, the home will eventually move too.

One of our favorite teachings of Jesus is found in Luke 6, where He gave us two examples of the foundations on which we can build our lives. (And remember—before beginning His ministry, Jesus was a carpenter.) First, let's look at His description of the wise builder.

> *I will show you what it's like when someone comes to me, listens to my teaching, and then follows it. It is like a person building a house who digs deep and lays the foundation on solid rock. When the floodwaters rise and break against that house, it stands firm because it is well built.*
> (vv. 47–48 NLT)

In Jesus's day, of course, the different types of material we use for foundations weren't available, so the best way to build a house was to set it on rock. Today, when the ground in an area is known to be soft or to expand and contract with extreme wet and dry conditions, one technique is to drill down into the earth and install piers—large concrete columns—under the slab. The house is then actually sitting on the piers and is not dependent on the ground below. Picture an elevated home built on the shoreline of a lake or ocean; you can see the piers it sits on that go through the water and deep into the earth. This is the same concept, but it's all in the ground.

Whether building on rock back then or on concrete buried in the earth today, when the floods rise and water is rushing, when the strong winds blow, the house stays put because the foundation is solid and secure.

Now let's look at the second builder Jesus talked about:

> *But anyone who hears and doesn't obey is like a person who builds a house right on the ground, without a foundation. When the floods sweep down against that house, it will collapse into a heap of ruins.*
> (v. 49 NLT)

Imagine going to check on your new home after construction has started and discovering that the builder is just setting your walls on the ground. Ridiculous, right? Everyone knows the first step is to lay a solid, level foundation. So, obviously, with no foundation or even a poor one, the same storm and flood that hit the wise builder would destroy this home.

We have to pay attention to the *two* steps Jesus gave:

1. Listen and hear Him.
2. Obey and put His words into practice.

Think about the millions of people who hear a sermon on any given Sunday at church. Do you think there's a difference in those who just hear versus those who hear and apply the message? Absolutely. A quick test is to ask someone on Monday morning what the pastor taught the day before.

Jesus was telling His followers (the twelve disciples and us) that obedience and the application of His words has to take place in order to create a solid foundation in the life of the believer.

James 1:22 takes this concept a step further, telling us that just listening to the Word without obedience is actually self-deception.

Do not merely listen to the word, and so
deceive yourselves. Do what it says.

When we choose to listen to and obey Jesus over our own will, the will of others, and the messaging of our culture, we choose His rock. We build our lives on the completed work of Jesus—His death, burial, and resurrection. Everyone else's opinions are shifting sand, but Jesus's words are the solid rock.

King David called the Lord his Rock in Psalm 18:2.

The Lord is my rock, my fortress and my deliverer;
my God is my rock, in whom I take refuge,
my shield and the horn of my salvation, my stronghold.

In good times and in bad, in the valley or on the mountaintop, in the distant country or back at home, His Word is the truth on which we can build our lives and stand.

Reflection

Is there any place in your life where you are hearing and listening but haven't yet obeyed and applied Jesus's words? Explain.

What are some specific ways you can pray *for* the rock of Jesus's words to impact the life of your prodigal *against* the shifting sand of the world?

Day 17

Living Your Life to Leave a Legacy

Music

Listen to today's song:

"So Good to Me"

Steve

Especially when we're young, when we are easily attracted to and distracted by so many things, we give little to no thought about our legacy—the family line we come from and especially the one we will one day create. Yesterday we talked about building a life foundation on rock or sand, and part of that process begins with where we start in our own families. Did we grow up on a shaky foundation or a solid one built on Jesus? While we know that can make a huge difference, it doesn't have to determine our destiny. So many people from horrible backgrounds go on to live amazing lives. Others who grow up in a solid and stable environment end up in disaster. Regardless, our legacy, both the one we come from and the one we are creating, is important. And it is especially crucial for the Christ-follower.

I can remember from a very early age how important being in church together was to my family. Because my Grandpa Williams and two of my uncles were Baptist preachers, the gospel was threaded throughout our lives. Our faith in Christ was a common topic at family gatherings. Grandpa, my parents, and two of my aunts would sing gospel songs and hymns quartet-style. I can remember how good the family harmony sounded. Nothing blends quite like blood relatives singing parts. I remember going to revivals and "singings" on Saturday nights and Baptist association meetings on Sunday afternoons to hear Grandpa Williams preach. Besides teaching the Word, he was an entertaining storyteller who had a gift for holding a crowd's attention. (Something that is also obvious in Zach's life today.)

Grandpa passed away in April 1974, and I surrendered my life to Jesus a year later in April 1975. I hope when I get to heaven, I can have a long conversation with Grandpa and Grandma. I would want to thank them for their legacy and the example they gave me. They had a huge impact on my life, even though I didn't realize it while they were alive. Also looking back, I'm amazed at how God took such good care of them as they lived by faith. They were truly a consistent testimony to me through their legacy.

In 1 Corinthians 3, Paul addressed some people in that church who were arguing over which leader to follow. In his explanation, Paul also told us how God works through the influential people in our lives to accomplish His work in us.

> *What, after all, is Apollos? And what is Paul? Only servants, through whom you came to believe—as the Lord has assigned to each his task. I planted the seed, Apollos watered it, but God has been making it grow. So neither the one who plants nor the one who waters is anything, but only God, who makes things grow. The one who plants and the one who waters have one purpose, and they will each be rewarded according to their own labor.*
> (vv. 5–8)

My family, especially my grandparents, planted the seeds of the gospel in my life. Along the way, they, along with others in our church, watered that seed. I knew in my early teens that God was drawing me, even though I resisted. But that was a result of the seeds of the gospel being watered by those Christ-followers around me. Then, finally, when Jenia and I saw the lives of our friends who came to Jesus, the harvest time came for us. The planting and years of watering paid off.

As Jenia and I began to follow Jesus, and especially after Zach and Amy came along, we did our best to listen and obey and to lead a godly life through the power of the Holy Spirit. We did our best to live out the teachings of the Word in our home, at work, and in our community. Just like Grandpa and Grandma Williams had done for me,

Jenia and I were now in that role of planting, watering, and praying for harvest in our own family. Our hearts were to carry on the powerful legacy of faith our families had given us. We hoped and prayed, even when the skies were dark and the storms were threatening, that, one day, our whole family would surrender to and follow Jesus. For the past several years, those prayers have changed to gratitude, and now Zach, Crystal, Amy, and Toby are carrying on the legacy of faith into the next generation.

Whether you come from a long line of Christians or you are the first one in your family to make a decision for Jesus, Satan wants your generation to be the last generation. That's why your mission of continuing to plant, water, pray, and believe is so crucial to your prodigal and the next generation of believers in your family. You can be the tipping point God works through to impact generations beyond you. You are on the journey of your own legacy today, of writing your family's story. And always remember, like Paul said, it is God who makes things grow.

To close, let's look at the next verses in today's passage as Paul followed Jesus's lead and used the building analogy, moving from his example of farming to construction.

> *For we are co-workers in God's service; you are God's field, God's building. By the grace God has given me, I laid a foundation as a wise builder, and someone else is building on it. But each one should build with care. For no one can lay any foundation other than the one already laid, which is Jesus Christ.*
> (vv. 9–11)

Reflection

Describe your family legacy regarding faith. How did that dynamic affect you?

If you are in communication with your prodigal, how can you best plant and water for Christ in his or her life? If you aren't in communication with them, pray for God to place Christ-followers around them who can and will.

Day 18

Your Counselor and Comforter

Music

Listen to today's song:

"Baptized"

Steve and Jenia

When we talk about the three Persons of the Godhead, the Trinity, we can understand the relationship and role of the Father and Son. But we can tend to misunderstand the Spirit. In the many denominations that Christianity has been divided into over the years, the Spirit is often polarized by being either completely ignored or badly abused. Some live the Christian life as if the Spirit doesn't exist, while others have created a very mystical, mysterious, and, at times, even exclusive image. While each person of the

Godhead is coequal and wholly God, each also has His own attributes and characteristics. Notice the distinct presence of each Person of the Trinity at Jesus's baptism.

> *As soon as Jesus was baptized, he went up out of the water. At that moment heaven was opened, and he saw the Spirit of God descending like a dove and alighting on him. And a voice from heaven said, "This is my Son, whom I love; with him I am well pleased."*
> (Matthew 3:16–17)

The Son was in the water and the Spirit was descending on Him while the Father's voice spoke from heaven. In John 14, Jesus promised that the Holy Spirit was going to come and reside in His followers after His resurrection and ascension to heaven.

> *And I will ask the Father, and he will give you another advocate to help you and be with you forever—the Spirit of truth. The world cannot accept him, because it neither sees him nor knows him. But you know him, for he lives with you and will be in you. I will not leave you as orphans; I will come to you. Before long, the world will not see me anymore, but you will see me. Because I live, you also will live. On that day you will realize that I am in my Father, and you are in me, and I am in you.*
> (vv. 16–20)

In 1 Corinthians 6:19, Paul said, *"Do you not know that your bodies are temples of the Holy Spirit, who is in you, whom you have received from God?"* When all this teaching comes together, we see that the Spirit who comes to live in us at salvation is the Spirit of Jesus, which explains His words *"you are in me, and I am in you."* Scripture describes the Holy Spirit in very personal terms. Here are ten examples, telling us that He

1. Teaches us what we need to know about God, from God (John 14:26);
2. Helps us in our weakness (Romans 8:26);
3. Intercedes for us when we pray (Romans 8:26);
4. Gives us access to God's power (Acts 1:8);
5. Offers us freedom (2 Corinthians 13:7);
6. Guides us into God's truth (John 16:12–13);
7. Convicts the lost of sin and continues to convict us when we sin (John 16:8–11);
8. Interprets spiritual truths to us (John 16:13–14);
9. Bears witness of Jesus (John 15:26); and
10. Seals or guarantees our redemption (Ephesians 4:30).

In Luke 11:11–13, Jesus was teaching His disciples when He said, *"Which of you fathers, if your son asks for a fish, will give him a snake instead? Or if he asks for an egg, will give him a scorpion? If you then, though you are evil, know how to give good gifts to your children, how much more will your Father in heaven give the Holy Spirit to those that ask him!"*

In this teaching, it's easy to focus on fish, snakes, eggs, and scorpions, but we shouldn't miss Jesus's promise of what the Father can bring us by and through the Holy

Spirit. Essentially, we receive so much more than the basic needs of life and certainly nothing evil in any way. In fact, in Galatians 5, Paul tells us the *"acts of the flesh"* (v. 19) are the ongoing sins characteristic of a life lived outside of the kingdom of God, but the *"fruit of the Spirit"* are gifts God produces in us that we can't on our own. Verses 22–23 say, *"But the fruit of the Spirit is love, joy, peace, forbearance, kindness, goodness, faithfulness, gentleness and self-control."* There is a vast difference in our love and God's love, our version of peace and His, and so on. Paul was talking about a unique heavenly brand of these qualities, ones you have to experience to understand.

We will first encounter the Holy Spirit when He convicts us of our sin and shows us our need for Jesus. Then, once we accept Christ by faith, the Holy Spirit enters our lives and indwells us for eternity. Throughout our days, He is that "still small voice" we sense in our spirits, a phrase we often hear to describe the whisper Elijah heard in 1 Kings 19:12. Also, as a Christian, this happens when we get a "gut feeling" about something that leads us to go deeper with God and live by faith. Jesus, the resurrected Son, now sits at the Father's right hand, with the Holy Spirit, dwelling within each believer to work in harmony and accomplish the Father's plans and purposes.

In your own life and the journey with your prodigal, the Holy Spirit is available to you 24/7. Listen for His voice and ask Him to guide you into God's truth. When you face tough days and hopeless feelings, trust Him to bring the help and hope you need.

Reflection

What has your understanding of the Holy Spirit been up to today? How does the Scripture you read today give you a better understanding of His role in your life?

Looking at the ten bullet points about what the Spirit does, which can help you as you navigate the relationship with your prodigal?

Day 19

Red like Crimson, White as Snow

Music

Listen to today's song:

"Flesh and Bone (We Remember)"

Steve and Jenia

When you hear the phrase "the blood of Jesus," what comes to mind? Maybe you think of a Bible story like when God through Moses turned the Nile River into blood. Or in Exodus where the law talks about blood from animal sacrifices. Or when Jesus sweat drops of blood in the garden before His trials began. Or where Paul talks about Christ's blood being shed for our sin. Maybe you think about taking Communion, where the wine or grape juice represents His blood. You may belong to a church that believes in transubstantiation, meaning the wine actually becomes Jesus's blood as you partake. Depending on your age, you might be reminded of classic hymns like "Nothing but the Blood of Jesus" or "Are You Washed in the Blood of the Lamb?" Regardless, as a Christian, you are aware that His blood holds a great deal of significance to your faith. Whatever your reference point about Jesus's blood, it's very important to have a true understanding and appreciation of how deep its power runs and all it has provided.

Everyone knows that blood is required for there to be human life, hence the term *lifeblood*. But the same is true in the spiritual sense. Throughout the Bible, blood is mentioned because of its importance and significance to God and therefore to us. In the story of Abraham and Isaac, after seeing Abraham's faithfulness, God provided an animal sacrifice, allowing a ram's blood to be shed instead of the son's. This theme of the covenant requiring spilled blood continues throughout the Old Testament into the New, right into the days of Jesus. However, the writer of Hebrews explained the transition that Christ brought.

> *But when Christ came as high priest . . . [he] did not enter by means of the blood of goats and calves; but he entered the Most Holy Place once for all by his own blood, thus obtaining eternal redemption. The blood of goats and bulls and the ashes of a heifer sprinkled on those who are ceremonially unclean sanctify them so that they are outwardly clean. How much more, then, will the blood of Christ, who through the eternal Spirit offered himself*

unblemished to God, cleanse our consciences from acts that lead to death, so that we may serve the living God! For this reason Christ is the mediator of a new covenant, that those who are called may receive the promised eternal inheritance—now that he has died as a ransom to set them free from the sins committed under the first covenant.
(9:11–15)

Jesus's blood provides for our cleansing, purification, forgiveness, redemption, justification (making us right with God), sanctification (transforming us into Christ's image), peace, and access to the throne of God. Paul spoke often about the blood of Christ in passages like Romans 3:25–26:

God presented Christ as a sacrifice of atonement, through the shedding of his blood—to be received by faith. He did this to demonstrate his righteousness, because in his forbearance he had left the sins committed beforehand unpunished—he did it to demonstrate his righteousness at the present time, so as to be just and the one who justifies those who have faith in Jesus.

The redemption that comes through the blood of Jesus opens the door to our fellowship with God, simply meeting with Him in close friendship. After Adam's fall in the garden, Christ has now made our relationship right with the Father. Jesus paid the price of sin by and through His blood to bring us back into intimate fellowship with God.

Another word for fellowship is *communion*. In what is known as the Last Supper, Jesus told His disciples as He held up the cup, *"Drink from it, all of you. This is my blood of the covenant, which is poured out for many for the forgiveness of sins"* (Matthew 26:27–28). Along with the bread that symbolizes His broken body, this is how we recognize that Jesus provided fellowship with God as we take Communion today. That is why observing this ordinance is so much deeper and more intimate than a mere religious ceremony. This fellowship with God allows us to recognize what Jesus did for us on the cross.

Imagine sitting around your dining table with your closest friends, sharing a meal as you visit, laughing, and talking about life. That is exactly the picture of what we have with God, along with our brothers and sisters in Christ. At the Savior's table of grace and forgiveness, you are always free to share your heart's deepest desires, hurts, concerns, and problems with the One who calls you friend (John 15:15). Because Jesus's blood has made the way.

Reflection

Was there any truth you learned about the blood of Jesus that you didn't yet know or understand? Explain.

In praying for your prodigal and his or her broken fellowship, how might today's passages help you as you pray?

Day 20

A Place for You

Music

Listen to today's song:

"To the Table"

Steve and Jenia

As a continuation from yesterday on the concept of fellowship made possible by Jesus's blood, today, we want to follow up with an amazing story of reconciliation and restoration from the Old Testament, a story that also involves a table.

In 1 Samuel 20, we're told about how David, the future king of Israel, and King Saul's son Jonathan had made a generational covenant between them: *"Jonathan said to David, 'Go in peace, for we have sworn friendship with each other in the name of the Lord, saying, 'The Lord is witness between you and me, and between your descendants and my descendants forever'"* (v. 42).

Later, Jonathan was killed in a battle with the Philistines, the nation David had confronted when he defeated Goliath. In that same battle, after Saul was critically wounded and surrounded by his enemies, *"he too fell on his sword and died"* (1 Samuel 31:5). When word got out to Saul's family that he was dead, they all fled in fear for their lives. A common practice from biblical days to medieval times was for the new king to hunt down and kill the old king's family to prevent any possible claim to the throne. But David, a man after God's own heart (Acts 13:22), was always a very different king who, with the exception of his sin with Bathsheba, sought to follow the Lord.

Remembering his covenant with Jonathan, King David inquired about any of Saul's remaining family. He was told about one of Jonathan's sons, Mephibosheth, who was living in obscurity. David was also informed that when the news came of Saul's death and the family was warned to flee, five-year-old Mephibosheth was grabbed up by his nurse. As she began to run, she stumbled and fell, causing permanent injury to his legs and feet, leaving him unable to walk. When word arrived that the king's men had come to take Mephibosheth back to David, he was likely stricken with fear, thinking he would be executed. But that's not at all what King David had in mind:

When Mephibosheth son of Jonathan, the son of Saul, came to David, he bowed down to pay him honor.

David said, "Mephibosheth!"
"At your service," he replied.
"Don't be afraid," David said to him, "for I will surely show you kindness for the sake of your father Jonathan. I will restore to you all the land that belonged to your grandfather Saul, and you will always eat at my table."
Mephibosheth bowed down and said, "What is your servant, that you should notice a dead dog like me?"
(2 Samuel 9:6–8)

Unable to work and living in a small, disrespected town with nothing left from his grandfather and father's estate, Mephibosheth revealed his true feelings about himself and his circumstances by calling himself *"a dead dog."* In that day, he would have had to crawl or be carried anywhere he needed to go. He lived in a desperate situation in a humiliated state. Imagine his shock and surprise when King David gave back everything that his family had owned, set up an income for him, and then, to top off the mercy and blessing, invited him to eat at his table every night—a table he likely would have to be carried to in order to join the fellowship.

And Mephibosheth, who was crippled in both feet, lived in Jerusalem and ate regularly at the king's table.
(2 Samuel 9:13 NLT)

That is the very picture of what King Jesus has done for us. While we deserve death because we, too, follow a family line of sin, He brings us before His throne, makes us His own, sets up a new life for us, and invites us to His table from now into eternity. Because of our past, our sin and brokenness, we are crippled spiritually. Yet, in our desperate and dependent state, Jesus carries us to His table to fellowship with Him.

Today, regardless of past failures, mistakes, and choices, God invites you to His table through a relationship with Jesus Christ. And on the days when you aren't sure if you have the strength to pull yourself up to the table, He will carry you there. For your prodigal, the table is also set and ready for him or her. Pray that any fear, like Mephibosheth had from his past, will be replaced by faith and hope, that they will decide to come home to a place at the table. Today's story is a beautiful picture of our heavenly Father's grace and mercy. He is the One who seeks and saves the lost (Luke 19:10). Jesus's finished work on the cross has set the table for all those who will come to Him by faith.

Reflection

What is one personal encouragement or truth you can take away from today's story for your own life?

How might understanding the offer of Christ's table and His ability to carry someone who lacks strength of their own empower your prayers for your prodigal?

Day 21

Fuel to Win the Fight

Music

Listen to today's song:

"Stand My Ground"

Zach

Out on the road, I meet people all the time who would not be sitting in front of me had it not been for the prayers of a parent, grandparent, spouse, family member, or friend. A constant, sincere prayer was a powerful expression of faith that God used to change someone's story.

When I was running from the Lord and chasing my own dreams, it was easy for me to think He wasn't involved with anything in my life. The lies I believed had to be demolished before I could see the truth. Today, I want to walk through some of the main things my parents did for me. But first, let's take a look at an intriguing event in the life of Daniel, the legendary champion of the lions' den:

Daniel 9:3 says, *"So I turned to the Lord God and pleaded with him in prayer and petition, in fasting, and in sackcloth and ashes."* Verses 4–19 give us Daniel's prayer. In verses 20–23, we're told:

> *While I was speaking and praying, confessing my sin and the sin of my people Israel and making my request to the LORD my God for his holy hill—while I was still in prayer, Gabriel, the man I had seen in the earlier vision, came to me in swift flight about the time of the evening sacrifice. He instructed me and said to me, "Daniel, I have now come to give you insight and understanding. As soon as you began to pray, a word went out, which I have come to tell you, for you are highly esteemed."*

In chapter 10, Daniel was told more:

> *Do not be afraid, Daniel. Since the first day that you set your mind to gain understanding and to humble yourself before your God, your words were heard, and I have come in response to them. But the prince of the Persian kingdom resisted me twenty-one days. Then Michael, one of the chief princes, came to help me, because I was detained there with the king of Persia. Now I have come to explain to you what will happen to your people in the future, for the vision concerns a time yet to come.* (vv. 12–14)

Daniel had been fasting and praying for over three weeks, and *"on the twenty-fourth day"* (v. 4) the vision came with the answer. This account in Daniel's life pulls back the curtain on the spiritual realm that we cannot see yet is obviously all around us. The important encouragement we can take from these verses is that God provided an answer right away, but a spiritual battle took place to try and stop the angel from delivering it to Daniel.

Think about this: What if a week in, even two weeks in, maybe on the twentieth day Daniel would have decided that God didn't care or wasn't listening? Or what if he started to assume that the answer was no? What if he had given up because he thought the answer should have already come? Daniel didn't know what was happening in the spiritual realm or how his prayer and fasting were impacting the supernatural, how his prayers in faith were being used as fuel to defeat the Enemy.

Well, if that is true for Daniel, it is also true for us. Your consistent prayer can win the fight for your prodigal. You don't know whether you're years, months, weeks, or only days away from victory, so don't give up. Remember, my parents prayed for me for over a decade.

If a loved one is caught up in a lifestyle that has him or her entrapped by the work of the Enemy, he will not give up easily. Therefore, for their sake, you can't give up easily either.

Here are four L's I know my parents practiced consistently:

- **Lift up your prodigal in faith.**

  As you pray, believe. Express your faith to God. When you don't have the words, ask for the Holy Spirit's help for what to pray.

- **Lead with patience.**

  In Paul's list about godly love in 1 Corinthians 13, he began with *"Love is patient"* (v. 4).

- **Love with grace.**

  1 Corinthians 13:5 says, *"[Love] does not dishonor others, it is not self-seeking, it is not easily angered, it keeps no record of wrongs."* That defines grace well.

- **Learn when to get out of God's way.**

  My parents had to eventually step back and allow God to deal with me. As a parent myself today, I know the pressure I can feel to have the answer for everything, even when I know I don't. Yet God's answers are not just better, they're perfect. Sometimes, we have to be quiet, step back, and give God the room He needs to work. To a prodigal or anyone we love, our voice cannot be louder than His and our actions can't get in the way of His.

Reflection

What can you learn from the passage about Daniel and how God answers prayer?

Which of the four action words—lift, lead, love, learn—do you most need to apply to your life for your prodigal?

Day 22

Results vs. Rest

• Music •

Listen to today's song:

"Washed Clean"

• Crystal •

After Zach and I came to Christ, turned our lives completely around, and began serving at our church in Arkansas, we were there every time the doors were open and dove headfirst into ministry. I also started being asked to share my testimony at women's events in the area. As I mentioned previously, my backstory before coming to Jesus is not pretty to hear and it's no fun to tell. In fact, it's painful. After a while, reliving all that anytime I spoke to a group began to get to me. It started to feel like too much of a show. At the peak of that season, I was also leading three different meetings as well as a women's life group. Bottom line—I was busy doing "good things."

As I began to reevaluate my life and pray for God's guidance, His answer came, telling me to not just slow down but actually stop and rest. He showed me I was doing too much, too soon, too fast. I remember He specifically said that "I couldn't reap when I was supposed to be sowing." With very clear direction, I decided to take a step back from serving at the church as well as from speaking. I went to the pastoral staff and explained my decision. Whenever someone is deep into leadership at a church and gives the appearance of "quitting," that rarely goes over well. It doesn't seem to matter if others believe you're listening to God or not, they just want you to keep going and giving. That's not being critical of any one church; it's far too common throughout our Western Christian culture. The best way I can express this is that it feels like results are more important than rest.

From there, I changed my focus and got involved at a center for abused women and in prison ministry. I found peace in those settings and felt comfortable again around a group of desperate, broken ladies who just needed to hear there is hope in Jesus, that help is possible and available, that they are not beyond His reach or too far gone for His love.

By the time the Lord launched Zach's Christian music career, I felt like He had used it all to prepare me for the life of being the wife of a touring artist. I've never had any angst about that like I did when he was out playing bars with the rock band. Life has been so very different from those days, and I don't worry about him being gone. In fact, I often tell him, "Go do what you gotta do." The fact is, I was always very supportive of him being a musician. The problem was never the music but the way we were living our lives. Today, there's purpose behind the music and it's *our* ministry.

My goal in sharing some of these experiences with you is this: God has shown me that so many of us as Christians feel like we have to keep doing, doing, doing and going, going, going for God. But the truth is, He just wants us to be with Him in the moment, doing what He calls us to do in the season we're in. After all, if we're supposed to be following Him, we have to learn how to rest in Him. He does not expect us to save the world, because that's what He does. And even if our whole life is spent helping only one person in Jesus's name, that might be the only thing God wanted us to do. And that's okay. To repeat, the Christian life is not about results for Him; it's about resting in Him.

Paul gave the Christians in Galatia (and us) a great challenge:

> *It is for freedom that Christ has set us free.*
> *Stand firm, then, and do not let yourselves be*
> *burdened again by a yoke of slavery.*
> (Galatians 5:1)

Our flesh and sin, our need for approval and affirmation, can drive us to become enslaved again by religious activity and "good things," when He died and rose again to free us up to live in and for Him. In Matthew 11:28–30,

Jesus told us what a life surrendered to Him is supposed to be like:

> *Come to me, all you who are weary and burdened, and I will give you rest. Take my yoke upon you and learn from me, for I am gentle and humble in heart, and you will find rest for your souls. For my yoke is easy and my burden is light.*

When we find ourselves weary and burdened by all the things we are trying to "do for God," it's time to remember the next part: *"and I will give you rest."* That means we have to stop and hand everything back over to Him. I realized that He doesn't want to watch me work for Him, He wants me to experience Him working through me. And trust me, there is a huge difference. Walking through life waiting for a prodigal is a tough road, so be sure you know that while you certainly want results, you also need to rest in Him, to trust in Him for His plan.

Reflection

Is there any way you relate to the struggles I (Crystal) shared with you today—past or present? Explain.

In walking through a prodigal story with your loved one, how might my (Crystal's) encouragement and the Bible passages today help you rest in Him when you so desperately want results?

Day 23

Specks and Logs

Music

Listen to today's song:

"Turn It Over"

Steve and Jenia

A difficult aspect of walking through a prodigal journey with a loved one is when we are blindsided by the people around us. Whether family, friends, neighbors, or church members, whether a person knows a little or a lot about our situation, someone's lack of maturity as a person and a Christian can make it challenging to navigate their attitudes and actions.

The very public pot-smoking incident that happened with Zach and his basketball teammates in high school was the first time we had been treated like outcasts in our own community. The most surprising part was the parents of the boys who were just as guilty but weren't punished, who said things like, "Oh my gosh, I can't believe Zach did that." Lots of pious finger-pointing went on. Life in a small town is great most of the time, but when something like that happens, you definitely feel like you're suddenly living in a glass house. And some folks decide to throw stones.

For many years, I (Steve) was involved with the worship team at church. When Zach started playing in local bars, our pastor, his wife, and the leaders in our church soon found out. While we didn't necessarily feel any condemnation directed toward us, we definitely could detect some judgment from our brothers and sisters in Christ toward Zach or Amy, which was very hard for us. Instead of feeling like most people had our backs, we felt abandoned. The irony later became how many of those same families ended up dealing with serious issues too, such as their kids' divorce and so on.

We began to understand that's why Zach and Amy didn't want to come to church in their young adult years. They felt judged, not loved. The very community that was supposed to be the example of God's grace was where they received condemnation. After Zach came to the Lord and turned his life completely around, his hair was still very long, way down his back. Around that same time, the church had hired us to do some work for about a week. Every time our new pastor and his wife came through, they never once spoke to Zach. They snubbed him, simply because of the way he looked. We must always remember 1 Samuel 16:7: *"People look at the outward appearance, but the* Lord *looks at the heart."*

Now, we aren't sharing these things to shame anyone; we're simply pointing out the sad truth that many people, even Christians, may be judgmental of your prodigal. Even your parenting or relationship with him or her can come under fire. And that hurts. But our calling from Christ is clear: We are to follow His example, not allowing bitterness or anger to infect our hearts but instead fostering forgiveness and reconciliation. No matter who we are or our role, we are all imperfect and have fallen short. Today, more than ever, people need to see God's grace displayed in Jesus's followers.

I (Jenia) have always had a harder time dealing with others' attitudes and actions, definitely more than Steve. But, over the years, walking through all we have endured, I had to learn to give grace to the people I know and to total strangers. And, as parents, we can sometimes struggle to show grace to our own kids, because we know that we raised them not to act in disobedient or disrespectful ways. That's why it is so important that we not point a finger at anyone else, because nobody's family, no one's life, is perfect. Jesus spoke clearly on this topic when He said,

> *Do not judge others, and you will not be judged. For you will be treated as you treat others. The standard you use in judging is the standard by which you will be judged. And why worry about a speck in your friend's eye when you have a log in your own? How can you think of saying to your*

> *friend, "Let me help you get rid of that speck in your eye," when you can't see past the log in your own eye? Hypocrite! First get rid of the log in your own eye; then you will see well enough to deal with the speck in your friend's eye.*
> (Matthew 7:1–5 NLT)

During that season, we also had to remind ourselves of Paul's teaching in Ephesians 6:12 when he said,

> *For our struggle is not against flesh and blood, but against the rulers, against the authorities, against the powers of this dark world and against the spiritual forces of evil in the heavenly realms.*

We knew that Satan was the author of accusation and condemnation. That's why we regularly prayed Jesus's authority over Zach and Amy's lives, telling the devil he couldn't have any hold on them. We constantly rebuked whatever we saw the Enemy trying to do in their lives. While Satan plotted evil, we believed God had good plans for them (Genesis 50:20).

In Matthew 23, Jesus was talking to the religious leaders about their judgment, condemnation, and self-righteous attitudes. Seven times He said *"Woe to you!"* and called them out for their sin. Here's verses 25–26:

> *"Woe to you, teachers of the law and Pharisees, you hypocrites! You clean the outside of the cup and dish, but inside they are full of greed and self-indulgence.*

Blind Pharisee! First clean the inside of the cup and dish, and then the outside also will be clean."

Remember as you deal with people on both ends of the spectrum—those who need grace and those who refuse to offer grace—that God loves them all and wants you to reflect His love and mercy. When someone appears to judge your prodigal or you, take it from us, this season will pass and God will ultimately have the victory. Every time you choose Jesus's way, you become more transformed into His image.

Reflection

Have you ever struggled with judging or condemning others? Explain.

Is there any situation where someone is judging your prodigal and/or you today? How can today's teaching and Scripture encourage you to better deal with this challenge?

Day 24

Praise Through the Pain

Music

Listen to today's song:

"Praise Opens Prisons"

Steve and Jenia

When you hear the words *praise* and *worship*, what comes to mind? Maybe you think about what happens at your church every Sunday morning before the sermon. Maybe you are reminded of the music you listen to at home, at work, or in the car. Over the past decade or so in the American church and Christian culture, "praise and worship" has come to represent a genre of music like country, rock, or hip-hop. That's exactly why we have to remind ourselves that praise and worship is simply about expressing our gratitude to God on a personal level. While that might include singing, it doesn't have to. But when we find ourselves thinking that expressing worship to God is relegated to Sunday morning or to a certain type of music, we have missed the point.

As you are walking through the journey with your prodigal, do you have days when you wake up feeling hopeless or broken? Are there nights when the circumstances seem futile and you start to doubt if anything will ever change? When we start to have those negative feelings, nothing seems worthy of our praise. Does the Enemy bring guilt or shame or raise questions of why you would ever worship the God who doesn't appear to be answering your prayers? How do we praise God, how do we worship Him, when we don't feel like we can?

In Acts 16, we find the story of a woman who was a slave of some owners who made a great deal of money from her satanic ability to be a "fortune teller." She began following Paul and Silas around Macedonia, shouting that they were servants of God who were telling people the way to be saved. While the statements were true, there must have been some mocking and condescension going on because, finally, Paul said to the spirit, *"In the name of Jesus Christ I command you to come out of her!"* (v. 18). When the evil spirit left her, her owners realized they had lost their income stream. The men took Paul and Silas to court and also incited a mob. They were beaten, thrown into prison, and had their feet locked in the stocks.

Now, what might any of us do in that situation? Demand an attorney? Complain to the guards? Call down curses on the people who caused the problem? Or maybe even get mad at God? Take a look at what Paul and Silas did.

About midnight Paul and Silas were praying and singing hymns to God, and the other prisoners were listening to them. (v. 25)

Both men were called by God, so they knew He had allowed this to happen. So, they started singing praise to Him! They began to worship God together. Let's be honest, that's not an option many of us, even as Christians, would consider. But what did their praise create?

Suddenly there was such a violent earthquake that
the foundations of the prison were shaken.
At once all the prison doors flew open,
and everyone's chains came loose.
(v. 26)

Imagine making the choice to start singing praise to God while you are in pain from being beaten and your feet locked into stocks. Suddenly, an earthquake shakes so powerfully that every prisoner's door flies open and every chain comes loose. Did Paul and Silas run for their lives?

The jailer woke up, and when he saw the prison doors open, he drew his sword and was about to kill himself

because he thought the prisoners had escaped. But Paul shouted, "Don't harm yourself! We are all here!"
(vv. 27–28)

The jailer knew his punishment for allowing prisoners to escape would be death, but so did Paul and Silas. They chose to put the jailer's life before their own and stayed for his sake. What happened next is amazing and miraculous.

The jailer called for lights, rushed in and fell trembling before Paul and Silas. He then brought them out and asked, "Sirs, what must I do to be saved?" They replied, "Believe in the Lord Jesus, and you will be saved—you and your household." Then they spoke the word of the Lord to him and to all the others in his house. At that hour of the night the jailer took them and washed their wounds; then immediately he and all his household were baptized. The jailer brought them into his house and set a meal before them; he was filled with joy because he had come to believe in God—he and his whole household.
(vv. 29–34)

The jailer was so blown away by Paul and Silas's choice to put his life before their own, particularly after he had treated them so harshly for no good reason, that he wanted the same peace and strength they had. Paul and Silas knew the small picture was their temporary suffering, while the big picture was a man and his family who needed salvation.

When Zach was going through the worst part of his rebellion, it seemed very much like he was trapped in a prison of his own making. But God got his attention one night through a worship song called "Redeemed." Out of his pain, he heard God's voice. Today, he sings God's praise, shares his story, and then watches Jesus open up the same prison doors that were opened for him—the spiritual, emotional, and mental prison that the Enemy still has so many locked up inside.

We want to challenge you to speak out and sing your praise to God as you pray for your prodigal's prison doors to be opened. You never know when "suddenly" He will shake the earth and provide a rescue.

• Reflection •

Regardless of what praise and worship has meant to you in the past, how can you begin to practice what we learned today from Paul and Silas, to praise to the point of God opening prison doors?

What are some ways that this story in Acts 16 can give you hope to believe in the spiritual release of your prodigal?

Day 25

Enduring Trials Through Steadfast Faith

Music

Listen to today's song:

"It's Good to Know"

Steve and Jenia

Over the past several decades, we've seen the constant development of new technology—the internet, social media, and the transition from all things analog to digital. Tasks that once took days now take only hours; those that once took hours can now be done in seconds. Yet our lives have become busier and, often, rushed and chaotic. As a result, we have become a very impatient and impulsive society. We want everything "on demand." These "improvements" and "advancements" have also left us with a lack of real, authentic community and an inability to stop and savor our accomplishments. We jump into relationships based only on a profile, we want what we don't have, we buy things we don't need and can't afford, and we take on more stress than we can handle.

What has all this done to our faith? Can we still decide to wait on something *only* God could bring about? How does the "I want it now" mindset affect belief in what He will bring about in time? The writer of Hebrews said, *"Now faith is confidence in what we hope for and assurance about what we do not see"* (11:1). When God called Abram, he was seventy-five years old. Imagine for a moment hearing this command today:

> *The* L*ORD had said to Abram, "Go from your*
> *country, your people and your father's household*
> *to the land I will show you.*
> *"I will make you into a great nation,*
> *and I will bless you;*
> *I will make your name great,*
> *and you will be a blessing.*
> *I will bless those who bless you,*
> *and whoever curses you I will curse;*
> *and all peoples on earth*
> *will be blessed through you."*
> (Genesis 12:1–3)

God promised to bless Abram and future generations through him, yet He was not specific in how that would happen. The immediate command was to "go" to an unknown land. If someone heard this same word from God today, what questions do you think might be asked? Likely some would be, "Okay, God, what address should I put into my maps?" "How many nights am I going to be gone?" "What clothes should I pack?" "Can I be back by the weekend? I've got big plans." "Any idea how much all this is going to cost, God? Things are tight right now." Sound familiar at all?

In Genesis 15:5–6, an amazing conversation occurred.

> *[God] took [Abram] outside and said, "Look up at the sky and count the stars—if indeed you can count them." Then he said to him, "So shall your offspring be." Abram believed the Lord, and he credited it to him as righteousness.*

Going back to Hebrews 11, more verses are dedicated to Abraham (Abram) and Sarah's faith than anyone else's. After reading Abram's response to God's promise, is it still possible today to wait for Him to act? Can we defeat our discouraged questions as to whether God will actually come through if we don't see an immediate answer? Almost twenty-five years after God's initial command, when Abram was ninety-nine, God appeared to him again and told him his name would become Abraham; that He would make him a "*father of many nations*" (Genesis 17:5); that Sarai's name would become Sarah, meaning "a mother of many nations"; and that she would give birth to a son named Isaac. Throughout the Bible, we read the phrase

"Abraham, Isaac, and Jacob" because everything happened just as God said. The faith that Abraham held on to for so many years, even through the trials and obstacles, allowed him to see and experience what he hoped for and what had been unseen.

We can always trust that God hears and will answer our prayers, but we may not always have an instant answer, just like Abraham's promise. Immediate answers might make it easier to trust God, but then we likely would not grow in our faith. But what about the times we feel like His answer is no? Well, that simply means He has better plans coming or wants to protect us from something we cannot see. God won't give us something that isn't His best for us.

James 4:3 explains another reason why we may be told no: *"When you ask, you do not receive, because you ask with wrong motives."* In 2 Corinthians 12:7–9, after Paul asked God three times to remove what he called *"a thorn in [his] flesh"* and *"a messenger of Satan"* that was tormenting him, God's reply was, *"My grace is sufficient for you, for my power is made perfect in weakness."* As Christians, we will eventually identify with Paul's spiritual attack and have to endure some kind of suffering. That's when we hold on to God's promises like Psalm 5:12, which says, *"Surely, Lord, you bless the righteous; you surround them with your favor as with a shield,"* and Psalm 84:11, *"No good thing does he withhold from those whose walk is blameless."*

Let's close today with three different versions of Hebrews 10:23, a powerful truth for us to hold on to.

Let us hold unswervingly to the hope we profess, for he who promised is faithful.

(NIV)

Let us hold tightly without wavering to the hope we affirm, for God can be trusted to keep his promise.

(NLT)

So let's do it—full of belief, confident that we're presentable inside and out. Let's keep a firm grip on the promises that keep us going. He always keeps his word.

(MSG)

• Reflection •

Have you ever looked back and been grateful that God *didn't* give you something you asked for? Something you later realized was His protecting you and giving you what's best for you?

The toughest part of walking through a prodigal season with a loved one is you don't know what is going to happen or when. How can today's message encourage you as you wait?

Day 26

New Life, New Song

Music

Listen to today's song:

"Everything Changed"

Steve and Jenia

In His conversation with Nicodemus in John 3, Jesus made reference to salvation as being born again, as in born anew. This means when a person places his or her faith in Christ, life is definitely going to change. For some, there is an overnight, radical difference and then the person settles into maturity. For others, it is slower and gradual, but it, too, is the beginning of a steady spiritual growth. A lot of factors can determine the speed and level of transformation. Yet everyone who truly surrenders to Jesus begins to look like Him—His character, qualities, and nature will start to show. The person's external life (actions and words) and internal life (attitudes and motives) will transform. Often in the world, we see change as outside in. With God, it is inside out. If Jesus is indeed in someone's life, He cannot and will not be hidden. Day by day, the way someone presents themselves will be affected by faith in Christ. Paul stated this so well in 2 Corinthians 5:17:

> *Therefore, if anyone is in Christ, the new creation has come: The old has gone, the new is here!*

This verse creates an if-then statement like many of us learned early on in math class: If *Christ*, then *new*. Where Christ resides, something new is present. It's not an option to change or a potential for it; there is evidence that a transformation is underway. For example, in Zach's case, all the truth that had been stored up in his heart since childhood quickly began to make sense to him once he had the nature of Christ inside. We saw his actions connect with belief when his spiritual eyes and ears were opened.

And when Zach started back up with his music, his songwriting changed. The veiled spiritual lyrics he sang previously were gone, and now the expression of his new nature was obvious and bold. The Message Bible has an interesting take on Psalm 144:9 that speaks to what we saw happen: *"O God, let me sing a new song to you, let me play it on a twelve-string guitar."* In Psalm 40:1–3, we hear the musician in David as he responded to God's rescue after bringing him to a new place.

I waited patiently for the L*ORD;*
he turned to me and heard my cry.
He lifted me out of the slimy pit,
out of the mud and mire;
he set my feet on a rock
and gave me a firm place to stand.
He put a new song in my mouth,
a hymn of praise to our God.
Many will see and fear the L*ORD*
and put their trust in him.

To use David's words, the new songs the Lord placed in Zach's mouth have led many to see and fear (give their awe and respect to) the Lord and put their trust in Him—a work that God continues to grow with each passing year. Watching God do such an amazing work, we were also given a new song, so to speak, as we witnessed the Father transforming our son's heart. For any of us, new songs are certainly welcome after years of praying and waiting for the old to change.

Once God begins making things new, you just never know what He might bring about. Another part of Zach's deliverance happened sixteen years after the incident in high school when the three of us met with his high school basketball coach. At some point over the years, I (Steve) had spoken to the coach, and he told me how he felt like the situation should have been handled differently. Long before this meeting, Jenia and I had forgiven him and put it behind us. Now, after Zach's salvation, that meeting was a big step for him as a part of his new life and finally putting his past behind him too. His coach has even come to a few of Zach's concerts and expressed how proud he is of the man Zach has become. More evidence of reconciliation that only God can provide.

In Revelation 21:4–7, we are told of the day when everything in heaven and on earth will be made new:

> *"'He will wipe every tear from their eyes. There will be no more death' or mourning or crying or pain, for the old order of things has passed away." He who was seated on the throne said, "I am making everything new!" Then he said, "Write this down, for these words are trustworthy and true." He said to me: "It is done. I am the Alpha and the Omega, the Beginning and the End. To the thirsty I will give water without cost from the spring of the water of life. Those who are victorious will inherit all this, and I will be their God and they will be my children."*

To encourage you as you wait and pray, watch for what might appear to be small changes that you see in your child or loved one. In Henry Blackaby's *Experiencing God*, a workbook that impacted us years ago, he taught, "People don't ask questions about spiritual matters unless God is at work in their lives. When you see someone seeking God or asking questions about Christianity, you are witnessing God at work." For us, this statement was very encouraging and helped us listen for any spiritual comment Zach made that he would have avoided before, any expression of a thought or emotion that had to be motivated out of spiritual conviction, any question asked to which God was the only possible answer. While these might be mere breadcrumbs on the trail, as Blackaby said, they can also be signs toward coming home.

Reflection

While it's tempting and easy to stay focused on your prodigal's old nature while waiting on them, how might today's verses keep you encouraged to pray for the new to come? Explain.

Thinking about your last conversation or interaction with your prodigal or the last information you received about them, is there anything you might have missed that is actually a sign of God drawing his or her heart toward Him? Explain.

Day 27

The Wealth of Wisdom

Music

Listen to today's song:

"Walk with You"

Steve and Jenia

Think for a moment about the people in your life you would describe as wise. The people around you who you know have wisdom. Now think about their choices that cause you to believe that to be true of them. If you thought of more than one person, do you see any common threads between them all? What is present in their lives that has given them wisdom? Maybe for some your answer would simply be age and life experience. For others, you could see a maturity about the way they approach life that you appreciate.

Solomon, David's son, who became king after his father died, was said to be the wisest man who ever lived. But where did that level of wisdom come from? 1 Kings 3 tells us about a conversation between God and Solomon. Try to put yourself in his shoes for a moment as you read.

> *At Gibeon the LORD appeared to Solomon during the night in a dream, and God said, "Ask for whatever you want me to give you."*
> (v. 5)

As Solomon began to form a humble answer, recognizing all that God had done for his father and himself, did he ask for greater riches? More gold and silver? Safety and security? A long life? Verse 9 gives the king's answer:

> *So give your servant a discerning heart to govern your people and to distinguish between right and wrong. For who is able to govern this great people of yours?*

Solomon asked nothing for himself; instead, he asked for God's help leading the people he was responsible for under His authority. This was not only selfless, but what? Yes. Wise. Mature. Admirable. God's response?

> *The Lord was pleased that Solomon had asked for this. So God said to him, "Since you have asked for this and not for long life or wealth for yourself, nor have asked for the death of your enemies but for discernment in administering justice, I will do what you have asked. I will*

give you a wise and discerning heart, so that there will never have been anyone like you, nor will there ever be." (vv. 10–12)

God went on to promise Solomon wealth, honor, and, if he would walk in obedience, a long life. But where did all this blessing begin? Solomon displayed wisdom in how he responded to God. In Solomon's book of Proverbs, we read,

The fear of the LORD is the beginning of knowledge,
but fools despise wisdom and instruction.
(1:7)

The word *fear* in this verse doesn't mean being scared of God. In fact, how could being afraid of God even be connected to knowledge and wisdom? Here, as in many places in the Bible, this word means awe, respect, trust, and reverence. See how you can interchange any of those four words with *fear* and it makes sense? First John 4:18–19 helps us better understand how God doesn't want fear to be a part of a relationship with Him: *"There is no fear in love. But perfect love drives out fear, because fear has to do with punishment. The one who fears is not made perfect in love. We love because he first loved us."* When you think of the people you love most and who love you, you mutually feel trust, respect, reverence, and a lack of fear.

As we grow closer to the Lord, we will be given more of His wisdom. As we become wiser in Him, we are drawn ever closer to Him. Giving reverence to God with respect and honor, reading His Word, and praying for His wisdom and understanding can give us strength to walk through any storm in life, including the season where we are waiting at the end of the road for our prodigal.

Reflection

How might gaining more wisdom and understanding from the mind of God help and support you in navigating your prodigal's journey?

How might you include today's Bible passages into your prayers for your prodigal? Include those today as you pray.

Day 28

From Tired and Weary to Running and Soaring

Music

Listen to today's song:

"Under My Feet"

Steve and Jenia

There were many days as we were walking through our kids' prodigal seasons that we felt like our strength was gone. It was easy in those times to feel like the defeats were mounting up beyond what we could handle. In those seasons, anyone can start to lose hope and feel powerless in every way. But we never gave up on those really tough days, because we recognized and confessed our weakness before

God. One of the most empowering passages in the Word that we often read and claimed is found in Isaiah 40:28–31:

Do you not know?
Have you not heard?
The Lord is the everlasting God,
the Creator of the ends of the earth.
He will not grow tired or weary,
and his understanding no one can fathom.
He gives strength to the weary
and increases the power of the weak.
Even youths grow tired and weary,
and young men stumble and fall;
but those who hope in the Lord
will renew their strength.
They will soar on wings like eagles;
they will run and not grow weary,
they will walk and not be faint.

We can choose to call on the One who never gets tired or weary. We can ask for His strength and power to become ours. We then place our hope not in ourselves but in the Lord, and we trust Him to help us get up and start walking again. God promises that if He renews our strength, He can help us to run and even soar. But going from tired and weary to running and soaring sounds amazing, and we wonder how such a transformation could ever happen.

Staying with this same concept, let's look at Ephesians 6:10, where Paul told us to *"be strong in the Lord and in his mighty power."* He went on to tell us how we can make the choice to be obedient and proactive in verses 13–17:

> *Therefore put on the full armor of God, so that when the day of evil comes, you may be able to stand your ground, and after you have done everything, to stand. Stand firm then, with the belt of truth buckled around your waist, with the breastplate of righteousness in place, and with your feet fitted with the readiness that comes from the gospel of peace. In addition to all this, take up the shield of faith, with which you can extinguish all the flaming arrows of the evil one. Take the helmet of salvation and the sword of the Spirit, which is the word of God.*

Paul used the tactical weapons of his day as a metaphor for the invisible, spiritual weapons we have available to us in the spiritual realm through Christ. Of course, a literal sword does no good when fighting a spiritual battle, and an actual breastplate won't save you from a demonic dart. But truth, righteousness, peace, faith, and salvation through the Spirit and the Word offer us everything we need to *"be strong in the Lord and in his mighty power."*

After detailing the protection and weapons we have at our disposal, in verse 18 Paul reminds us of the most precious power we have for both offense and defense.

> *And pray in the Spirit on all occasions with all kinds of prayers and requests. With this in mind, be alert and always keep on praying for all the Lord's people.*

Because we have this incredible access to God, we need to be sure that darkness never wins in our lives simply because it outlasts us. We mustn't grow weary, lose faith, or stop fighting. Remember all the Rocky movies? He was never bigger or stronger than any of his opponents. In fact, most of them were huge. So how did Rocky always eventually win by the final fight of every movie? He outlasted them. He was the only one with any strength left to throw a punch.

While Jesus has already dealt darkness the final blow and the ultimate war is won, Scripture tells us that we have to stand firm in our daily battles and pray for Him to help us overcome. Our part, our obedience, our cooperation matters to Him. The only possible explanation for this is that He desires the deep relationship that is formed as we fight alongside Him. Until God rings the final bell for this earth, we are very much in a continual fight for the souls of mankind. Today, in your prayers for your prodigal and your own life, commit to following Paul's challenge in Ephesians 6 to be the one who decides to stand firm in Christ.

Reflection

Based on the Scriptures today, how do you think your choices and faith affect your ability to stand firm and see God's victory?

How might you use Paul's words in Ephesians 6 in a prayer for your prodigal?

Day 29

Name Above All Names

Music

Listen to today's song:

"That'll Preach"

Steve and Jenia

Before Zach closes out the final day tomorrow, we wanted our last time with you to be focused on the One who has changed all our lives, the One to whom we owe all our praise and gratitude—Jesus. If you are new in your walk with Him or maybe you're trying to do a reset in your spiritual life, the book of John is a great place to get back into the Word. John's Gospel and Paul's letter to the Romans give us a solid foundation in Christian doctrine and help us understand what this new life is all about.

Throughout the book of John, leading up to Jesus's arrest, trials, and crucifixion, we are provided many descriptions of Him, some from the writer himself and some quoted directly from the Lord. The first verses of his gospel start off by making sure we understand that Jesus was *"with God in the beginning"* (1:2) and was fully involved in creation: *"Through him all things were made; without him nothing was made that has been made"* (v. 3). Let's walk through the book and focus on other verses that declare and describe Jesus's identity.

Jesus is the

- Life, as explained in the verses above (v. 4).
- Light for all mankind who came into the world to shine into and overcome the darkness of Satan and a sinful, broken world (vv. 4–5, 9).
- Adopter who came to give all who would believe in Him the right to become children of God (vv. 12–13).
- One who came in the flesh as a man to live among us to show the Father's glory, grace, and truth (v. 14).
- Lamb of God who takes away the sins of the world (vv. 29, 35).
- Miracle Maker (2:1–11; 6:1–24).
- Fulfillment of prophecy (2:13–22).
- Rabbi, Teacher, and Baptizer (3:1–26; 7:14–39).
- Savior (3:16–17; 4:42).
- Water of Life (4:13–14).
- Healer (4:43–54; 5:1–15; 9:1–12).
- Son of God (5:16–30).

- Bread of Life (6:33–59).
- Protector (ch. 8).
- Good Shepherd and the Gate (10:1–18).
- Giver of full and abundant life (10:10).
- Resurrection and the Life (11:25).
- King (12:12–15).
- Son of Man (12:23–34).
- Example and Servant-Leader (13:1–17).
- Way, the Truth, and the Life (14:6).
- Peace (14:27).
- Vine through which God's fruit may be produced in us as His branches (15:1–8).
- Friend (15:12–17).

This list gives us plenty of evidence to see that after Jesus had accomplished His mission on earth, He left us with everything we need. In Christ, we lack nothing. In Christ, we have access to all the good gifts of God. Finally, His Spirit—the Advocate, the Comforter—lives within us to *"teach you all things and will remind you of everything I have said to you"* (14:26) and to *"guide you into all the truth. He will not speak on his own; he will speak only what he hears, and he will tell you what is yet to come. He will glorify me because it is from me that he will receive what he will make known to you"* (16:13–14).

The good news of the gospel is that no one is excluded from God's offer of salvation. His love will never demand that anyone receive Him, but He will make certain everyone has the opportunity. God has made provision for the whole world, so that no one is beyond His mercy. First John 2:2

states, *"He is the atoning sacrifice for our sins, and not only for ours but also for the sins of the whole world."* John goes on to say, *"This is how God showed his love among us: He sent his one and only Son into the world that we might live through him. This is love: not that we loved God, but that he loved us and sent his Son as an atoning sacrifice for our sins"* (4:9–10).

When you are struggling in your own life or as you walk with a loved one through their prodigal journey, constantly remind yourself who Jesus is to you. Look through these verses and other places in Scripture to find who He is to you on any particular day, whether as Father, Friend, Healer, Water in a spiritual desert, or Bread when you are starving for hope. Jesus offers everything you need. You only have to seek Him. He will be there to hold and help you as you wait at the end of the road.

Reflection

Which name or description of Jesus in the book of John most resonates with you right now? Explain.

Which name or description of Jesus in the book of John do you most feel you need to appeal to as you pray for your prodigal? Share your answer in a prayer.

Day 30

The Road to Jesus

Music

Listen to today's song:

"Plan for Me"

Zach

When I share my story, I always try to be clear that I never want to glorify anything I did in my past. I am not proud of the choices I made while trying to run away from God. Mine is a cautionary tale to anyone who will listen, to not go down the broad road Jesus spoke of in Matthew 7:13 that leads to destruction. But in the parable of the prodigal son, Jesus also mentioned a road—the road that leads back to the Father, to forgiveness, to restoration, to salvation. That's the only right road to take, the way to the Father that Jesus called Himself in John 14:6. I will tell anyone from firsthand experience that it's not worth the heartache for you and your loved ones to make any other choice.

After hearing my story, a lot of people tell me, "Zach, I don't have a testimony like yours. I came to Jesus early in life and have been walking with Him ever since." Every time, I respond the same: "No, please don't say that. You have the *best* kind of testimony. Because you didn't have to go through anything hard or hurt anyone to realize your need for Jesus. The sooner anyone comes to Him, the better."

I 100 percent believe the very reason God allowed me to survive and live through everything I did was so I can now share with people how good He is, how much He loves us, and how He can protect us. No one can walk up to me and say, "Yeah, Zach, but you don't understand how bad *my* life is." While I may not have lived someone's specific situation, I can relate to most everyone, even people in prison, to those who feel like the nobodies of this world. I can look those folks in the eye and say, "I get it. I've been there. I've done it. But I'm also on the other side today to tell you there's a better way to live."

One of the struggles a past like mine can create is making it hard to understand how God can so easily forgive. Especially when I still willfully disobey Him, when I fail and mess up, how can He let that go? Once you truly understand the depth, the depravity, and the nature of your sin, you realize how you can abuse His grace. Crystal and I talk about that all the time. I often pray, "Why did You choose to use me for this? Why did You pick me out of everyone for this calling? To work through me to write these songs and sing to people?" While I realize the responsibility, I also know there's no real explanation for it; that's just how He works. Ephesians 2:8–10 says,

> *God saved you by his grace when you believed. And you can't take credit for this; it is a gift from God. Salvation is not a reward for the good things we have done, so none of us can boast about it. For we are God's masterpiece. He has created us anew in Christ Jesus, so we can do the good things he planned for us long ago.*
> (NLT)

Yet anytime I get to see someone understand the gospel for the first time, when someone realizes there's a place where no one cares what they've done or where they've been, to watch a person receive the love of Christ, that's always special to witness. While being on the road can be hard, that part of my calling never gets old.

I am more grateful every day to my parents and the people who pointed me to Jesus, who planted the seeds of the gospel in my life. I would never have been able to accomplish any of the things I have without God working in and through those He placed around me.

When we hand our mess of a life over to God, He can take all the broken pieces and put something together we never dreamed possible. But He won't do that until we surrender everything to Him. Then, once we start to experience God putting life back together, we can begin to understand why He has allowed the things He has in our lives.

With this being your final day in this devotional, I pray that my parents' wisdom and encouragement, along with Crystal's and my testimony, have given you hope and offered you some biblical, practical support as you walk out this journey with your prodigal loved one. We know the pain you feel. We understand the questions you have. We get the struggle. Yet, more than anything, we know the God we all serve and how He can accomplish the impossible, no matter how challenging any circumstance may be.

Our family echoes the apostle Paul's blessing over the Colossians for you and your family:

Let the peace of Christ rule in your hearts, since as members of one body you were called to peace. And be thankful. Let the message of Christ dwell among you richly as you teach and admonish one another with all wisdom through psalms, hymns, and songs from the Spirit, singing to God with gratitude in your hearts. And whatever you do, whether in word or deed, do it all in the name of the Lord Jesus, giving thanks to God the Father through him.
(Colossians 3:15–17)

Reflection

Like I (Zach) shared with you today, do you sometimes struggle with believing God can work in and through your life? Explain.

Personalize Colossians 3:15–17 and pray those words for your prodigal.

WRAP-UP REVIEW

This final exercise is to help you look back over the entire book and all your hard work in order to gain as much insight and wisdom as you can in what God is speaking to you and how He may be leading you.

1. Was there a new truth (or truths) that God revealed to you in one of the days? Explain.

2. Was there anything God revealed to you that you know you need to work on and apply?

3. Was there a particular Bible verse or passage that spoke to your heart? How did it influence you?

4. Is there any specific step of obedience that you sensed God is calling you to make?

5. How have these thirty days most helped you in praying and believing for your prodigal to come home?

BEGINNING A RELATIONSHIP WITH GOD THROUGH JESUS CHRIST

If at any point as you went through this devotional you had the question "So how do I begin a relationship with God?" here is a simple explanation of the gospel of Jesus Christ.

There is a God-shaped hole, an emptiness, inside each of us. We each try to fill this void in our own way. We cannot see on our own that God Himself is the answer to our emptiness. His Spirit has to help us.

The Bible defines sin as attitudes, thoughts, and actions that displease God. Every person since Adam and Eve disobeyed God in the garden has had this problem. Even if we try really hard to be "good," we can never earn the perfect righteousness of a holy God (Matthew 5:48).

In Paul's letter to the Roman church, he created a pattern that lays out a path to salvation in Christ. For millions of people, these simple yet profound truths have led to new life. Take your time and read these now. Remember, these are personal to you as God makes His offer of new life.

For ever since the world was created, people have seen the earth and sky. Through everything God made, they can clearly see his invisible qualities—his eternal power and divine nature. So they have no excuse for not knowing God. Yes, they knew God, but they wouldn't worship him as God or even give him thanks. And they began to think up foolish ideas of what God was like. As a result, their minds became dark and confused.
(Romans 1:20–21 NLT)

We are made right with God by placing our faith in Jesus Christ. And this is true for everyone who believes, no matter who we are.
For everyone has sinned; we all fall short of God's glorious standard.
Yet God, in his grace, freely makes us right in his sight. He did this through Christ Jesus when he freed us from the penalty for our sins.
(Romans 3:22–24 NLT)

But God showed his great love for us by sending Christ to die for us while we were still sinners.
(Romans 5:8 NLT)

For the wages of sin is death, but the free gift of God is eternal life through Christ Jesus our Lord.
(Romans 6:23 NLT)

If you openly declare that Jesus is Lord and believe in your heart that God raised him from the dead,

you will be saved. For it is by believing in your heart that you are made right with God, and it is by openly declaring your faith that you are saved.
(Romans 10:9–10 NLT)

For "Everyone who calls on the name of the LORD will be saved."
(Romans 10:13 NLT)

For everything comes from him and exists by his power and is intended for his glory. All glory to him forever! Amen.
(Romans 11:36 NLT)

Countless people have begun a relationship with God through Jesus Christ after reading Paul's words guiding us to salvation. This is the truth of the gospel—the good news. But God gives you the choice. If you know you are ready to begin a relationship with Him right now, while there are no magic words or formulas for receiving God's gift of salvation, we have included a simple prayer for guidance:

Dear God, I know I am a sinner and need Your forgiveness. I now turn from my sins and ask You into my life to be my Savior and Lord. I choose to follow You, Jesus. Please forgive my sins and give me Your gift of eternal life. Thank You for dying for me, saving me, and changing my life. In Jesus's name, amen.

For I am not ashamed of this Good News about Christ. It is the power of God at work, saving everyone who believes—the Jew first and also the Gentile.
(Romans 1:16 NLT)

If you prayed the prayer or one on your own to place your faith in Christ, or if you have more questions, we encourage you to talk to a pastor, priest, or mature Christ-follower about this significant spiritual decision.

ABOUT THE AUTHORS

Steve and Jenia Williams were high school sweethearts who have been married for 53-plus years. After surrendering their lives to Jesus in 1975, they chose to build their home on His truth. In 1978, Zach was born in Pensacola, Florida while Steve attended Liberty Bible College. Amy came along in 1980 after the family moved back home to Arkansas.

Steve worked in construction and owned his own drywall business for 45 years before retiring in 2022. Jenia was a hairdresser, then a nurse's aide. In 1985, she pursued a degree in nursing. After graduating in 1989, she worked until retirement in 2018.

Steve was involved in leading worship and playing guitar at church for over 25 years. Today, they both volunteer in the Celebrate Recovery program at their church.

Steve and Jenia have 7 grandchildren, ranging from teens to young adults. Steve enjoys sports and gardening, while Jenia loves arts and crafts, acrylic/watercolor painting, sewing, baking, and cooking. Both are passionate about

God's Word, prayer, and seeing people experience Jesus in the same way He changed their lives.

Zach Williams has become one of CCM's leading artists and songwriters by carving a niche with his singular blend of southern rock, country, and faith-filled songwriting, which quickly awarded him his first GRAMMY Award® with his debut album, 2017's *Chain Breaker*. *Rescue Story* followed in 2019, and in 2022 Zach returned with his third full-length album, *A Hundred Highways*. Zach and his family live near Nashville, Tennessee.

Connect with Zach

You've experienced the devotional, now read Zach's memoir.

Rescue Story: Faith, Freedom, and Finding My Way Home

Get the book by scanning the QR code with your smartphone:

Access Zach's music, videos, tour schedule, merch store, and website by scanning this QR code with your smartphone